A FRESH START
FOR AMERICA

Policy Addresses of George W. Bush

Published by Bush for President, Inc.
Post Office Box 1902
Austin, Texas 78767

Printed in the United States of America

Photography on pages 6, 26, 78, 126, 148, 164, 178
by Charles Ommaney
Photography on page 50 by Brian Vincent
Photography on page 102 by Bill Records
Biography Photo by Gray Hawn

For current policy information visit www.georgewbush.com

TABLE OF CONTENTS

Preface		iv
1	**Education: No Child Left Behind**	7
	Position Paper	18
	What Others Say	25
2	**Education: A Culture of Achievement**	27
	Position Paper	39
	What Others Say	49
3	**Education: The True Goal of Education**	51
	Position Paper	62
	What Others Say	72
4	**The Duty of Hope: Armies of Compassion**	79
	Position Paper	88
	What Others Say	101
5	**A Tax Cut with a Purpose**	103
	Position Paper	113
	What Others Say	124
6	**Defense: A Period of Consequences**	127
	Position Paper	138
	What Others Say	146
7	**Foreign Policy: A Distinctly American Internationalism**	149
	Priorities	162
	What Others Say	163
8	**Agriculture: The Heart of our Economy**	165
	Position Paper	170
	What Others Say	176
9	**High Tech: Taking the Side of Innovation**	179
	Position Paper	187
	What Others Say	192
10	**Positions Taken on the Issues**	194
11	**George W. Bush Biography**	207

PREFACE

"If you don't know where you are going," said Yogi Berra, "chances are you will end up someplace else." The following proposals and speeches – given between July and December, 1999 – begin to outline where I will go as President. On issues from the education of our children to the defense of our nation, I have set out to combine a vision with a set of specific tasks.

Not every topic, at this stage of the campaign, is covered in these addresses. But they reveal my priorities. And I hope they also demonstrate a distinctive approach to leadership and governing.

- Government should be carefully limited, but forceful and energetic within the bounds of its responsibilities. It should do a few things, and do them well.

- Many of my proposals reflect approaches I tested and refined in Texas. Around the country, over the last decade, Republican governors and mayors have been solving problems of crime, welfare dependence and educational failure that once seemed hopeless. I want to bring this kind of positive, creative, can-do conservatism to the White House.

- Policy proposals should be detailed, realistic and responsible. They must be more than empty political symbolism, without a chance of becoming law. They must add up to a governing agenda.

- Republicans must offer hope and help to everyone in our society – to children in failed schools, to neighborhoods bypassed by prosperity, to single mothers and working families. We must reflect and inspire the moral idealism of our country – a commitment to basic fairness and the common good.

- The moral values of our tradition – responsibility, faith and family – should be defended without apology. Not only because they are true and right, but because they make our society more just and compassionate.

- And all of these high goals depend on rebuilding our nation's military strength and effectively pursuing our nation's interests abroad – defending a peace favorable to freedom.

I have done my best to define, not just an agenda for a campaign, but an agenda worthy of a great nation. I hope you will consider these words, examine my proposals, and join me in a great cause.

George W. Bush

1

Education:
No Child Left Behind

Latin Business Association Luncheon
Los Angeles, CA

September 2, 1999

It is good to be with you - with men and women who are building the new economy of California.

We are witnessing a Latino economic miracle - un milagro económico. There are now 440,000 Latino businesses in Southern California. They generate $47 billion in sales each year. Latino businesses are the largest and fastest growing part of the small business community in this region. When half of the new businesses in Los Angeles are Latino-owned, this is no longer a niche market. It is the mainstream of our economic hopes.

This marks a new era - a permanent revolution - in California, and in many other places, including my state of Texas. An era in which the Latino market will demand the attention of our whole economy. An era in which our prosperity is as broad and diverse as our nation. This community has saved and worked and struggled. And now it has arrived.

The health of the Latino business community is reflected in the health and growth of this organization - the largest association of Latino entrepreneurs in the state. The Latin Business

Association is doing well, and it is also doing good work by helping other entrepreneurs realize their dreams.

I am here with you today because you are leaders and because you embody the permanent hope, the durable dream, of this nation: to build a better life for ourselves and our children.

I am an optimist. I believe that the next century will be a time of incredible prosperity - if we create an environment where entrepreneurs like you can dream and flourish. A prosperity sustained by low taxes, unleashed by lighter regulation, energized by new technologies, expanded by free trade. A prosperity beyond all our expectations, but within our grasp.

Yet all around this country, I have argued that prosperity must have a higher purpose. The purpose of prosperity is to make sure the American dream touches every willing heart. The purpose of prosperity is to leave no one out - to leave no one behind.

This noble goal will remain a distant goal until our nation fulfills a solemn pledge: to educate every child. In coming weeks, I plan to talk about the safety of our schools, the character of our children, the education standards we should set, and the accountability we should expect.

But I want to start where educational failure has its highest price. I want to begin with disadvantaged children in struggling schools, and the federal role in helping them. Their voices are not the loudest in our education debates. But we owe them the pride and promise of learning. Our new economy - requiring higher and higher skills - demands it. And so does our conscience. No child in America should be segregated by low expectations...imprisoned by illiteracy...abandoned to frustration and the darkness of self-doubt.

National wealth is a worthy goal. But what would it profit our nation to gain the whole world and lose our own children?

In response to this challenge, the last several years have been a time of bold change in education. A drizzle of innovation has become a flood of reform - a great movement of conscience and hope. A movement of parents and political leaders, voters and educators, hungry for high standards, tough accountability and real choices. Five years ago, only eight states had charter school laws. Today there are 35. A few years ago, no state had school-by-school report cards. Now there are at least three dozen.

Unlike past fads and fashions, these reforms are proving that public education can be improved - swiftly and dramatically.

I have seen it with my own eyes. The skeptics of education reform should visit KIPP Academy in Houston - a charter school that mainly serves the children of Latino immigrants. KIPP refuses to accept the "high-risk" label, demanding high standards and hard work. Children have nine-and-a-half-hour days, class on Saturday and two hours of homework a night. The director promises, "If you're off the bus, you're working." And it is an incredibly cheerful and hopeful place. When you go there, you can see the light of ambition and discovery in young eyes. You can sense the self-esteem that comes from real accomplishment. After one year at KIPP, nearly 100 percent of students pass our state skills test in math and reading, making it the number one public middle school in all of Houston.

Or look at the Bennett-Kew Elementary School near here in Inglewood. A school I recently visited. A haven of hope. Nearly 8 in 10 students are disadvantaged, but it posts some of the strongest test scores in Los Angeles County. It teaches mastery of reading in kindergarten, and promotion in every grade level is tied to achievement. The principal explains: "We believe all children can learn. And they do."

Why do some schools work in places where so many schools fail? We can see the emerging outlines of an answer. In places all around our country, like Texas and North Carolina and California and Virginia and Massachusetts, governors and parents and teachers - Republicans and Democrat and none-of-the-above - are embracing reforms and calling for excellence.

- First, schools must have a few clear, measurable goals, focused on basic skills and essential knowledge. Education is about results, not theories; about knowledge, not intentions. "If you don't know where you are going," said Yogi Berra, "chances are, you'll end up someplace else." When I became Governor of Texas, we had 48 separate educational goals - which meant that a school might achieve 40 goals, and still not teach children to read. We reduced that number to four goals: excellence in reading, math, science and social studies.

- Second, we must measure to make sure standards are met. In Texas, we measure. We test because parents must know if education is taking place. We test because informed parents become more involved. We test because children must get the help they need before they are lost in the system. We test because hard data allows teachers and principals to examine their methods and change their direction. Measurement makes some people nervous. But without tests, there is no pressure for progress.

- Third, effective reform requires accountability. Someone should be praised when schools succeed, and someone must be responsible when schools fail. As much as 37 percent of school principals in low-performing Texas schools have been replaced or retired each year, because citizens and parents have refused to accept failure.

- Fourth, accountability is empty without local control of schools. It is essential to align responsibility and accountability at the local level; to separate them provides a convenient excuse for failure - just blame the central office. Higher standards demand broader flexibility.

- Finally, we must recognize the essential role of competition in achieving our goals - competition from charters and parental choice and home schooling. All monopolies are slow to reform when consumers have no power to express their frustration. In education, parents who have options have influence. When the Children's Scholarship Fund recently offered 40,000, privately funded, partial scholarships to poor children, it received a million applications. One million - even though parents had to match this help with money of their own. This was a direct challenge to failing public schools - and should be a motive for change. Charter schools are another good example. When they passed in Texas, critics charged they'd be a haven for fleeing Anglo students. In reality, 78 percent of students enrolled in Texas charters are minorities. These diverse, creative schools are proof that parents from all walks of life are willing to challenge the status quo if it means a better education for their children.

These reforms are proving their worth, but the movement I am talking about requires more than sound goals.

It requires a mindset that all children can learn, and no child should be left behind. It does not matter where they live, or how much their parents earn. It does not matter if they grow up in foster care or a two-parent family. These circumstances are challenges, but they are not excuses. I believe that every child can learn the basic skills on which the rest of their life depends.

Some say it is unfair to hold disadvantaged children to rigorous standards. I say it is discrimination to require anything less - the soft bigotry of low expectations. Some say that schools can't be expected to teach, because there are too many broken families, too many immigrants, too much diversity. I say that pigment and

11

poverty need not determine performance. That myth is disproved by good schools every day. Excuse-making must end before learning can begin.

This reform movement also requires a different mindset in politics. Education is too important to have a strategy of divide and conquer. Unless parents and principals, teachers and academics, Republicans and Democrats can find common purposes, reform will fail. I have worked closely with both parties in my state, because I know that if we set out to score partisan points, we will never solve problems. If we do not share credit for progress, all of us deserve the blame for failure.

In Texas, we are proud of our results. We have more than 7,000 public schools, as diverse as any in America. Since 1994, the number of minority children passing our state skills test jumped from 38 percent to 69 percent. Between 1994 and 1999, Hispanic eighth graders posted a 40 point gain on our math exam. African-American fourth graders have better math skills in Texas than in any state in the country.

A lot of people deserve credit - students and parents and teachers and principals and legislators - and I am proud of my part. Education has been and will be a priority for me. I will carry a passion for high standards and high hopes to the highest office in the land.

For all the advances some states have made, too many children are being left behind. We are nation where a majority of fourth graders in our cities can't read or understand a simple children's book. Where ninth-graders too often have fourth-grade reading skills. Where the achievement gap between rich and poor, Anglo and minority, is wide - and, in some cases, growing wider still.

It is a scandal of the first order when the average test scores of African-American and Latino students at age 17 are roughly the same as white 13-year-olds. Whatever the cause, the effect is discrimination. Children who never master reading will never master learning. They face a life of frustration on the fringes of society. Large numbers turn to crime and end up in prison. This is a personal tragedy. More and more, we are divided into two nations, separate and unequal. One that reads and one that can't. One that dreams and one that doesn't.

For many years the federal government has tried to close this gap of hope - armed with good intentions and billions of dollars. But sacks of money and the best of motives have made little difference in the performance of disadvantaged children.

At last count, the federal government had 760 different education programs operating within 39 different agencies, boards and commissions. Each was launched as a step toward reform. But the actual results are usually a mystery, because no one measures them. The only thing we know for sure is that federal money comes with a lot of regulations and paperwork. By one estimate, this consumes about 50 million hours each year - the equivalent of 25,000 full-time employees just to process forms.

The problem here is that failure never turns to wisdom. New layers of federal mandates and procedures have been added to the old, until their original purpose is long forgotten. It is a sad story. High hopes, low achievement. Grand plans, unmet goals.

My administration will do things differently.

We do not have a national school board, and do not need one. A president is not a federal principal, and I will not be one.

The federal government must be humble enough to stay out of the day-to-day operation of local schools, wise enough to give states and school districts more authority and freedom, and strong enough to require proven performance in return. When we spend federal money, we want results - especially when it comes to disadvantaged children.

Today, I want to outline three reforms to help ensure that no child is left behind:

We will start by funding only what works in education - only those methods and ideas that prove their power to close the achievement gap. We need good, reliable, scientific information on the best methods of teaching. What the federal government sponsors, however, is often sloppy and trendy, focusing on self-esteem over basic skills. My administration will require every federal program - in teacher training, curriculum research, school safety - to prove results. If it can't, we will shift that money into a program that is using it wisely. No federal education program will be reauthorized merely because it has existed for years. It is more important to do good than to feel good.

Take, for example, teaching children to read and comprehend English. If a good immersion program works, I say fine. If a good bilingual program works to teach children English, we should applaud it. What matters is not the varying methods, but the common standards and goals. The standard is English literacy. The goal is equal opportunity. All in an atmosphere where every heritage is respected and celebrated.

Esta propuesta la he llamado "Inglés y Más," porque yo me opongo al "Inglés solamente." "Inglés solamente" significa "solo yo," sin tomar en cuenta a otros. "Inglés y Más" significa "todos nosotros, pero juntos." Children - of any background - should not be used as pawns in bitter debates on education and immigration, or punished to make a broader political point.

There is one area where the teaching research is definitive: The best way to teach children to read is phonics. No new theory or method has ever improved on it, as Californians know better than anyone. The National Institutes of Health - in the kind of rigorous research we need - has proven that phonics works, and that children can learn to read much earlier than we assumed.

But we must take this a step further. We now have compelling evidence that children ages three and four can begin to read. We also have a massive Head Start program, serving 840,000 disadvantaged children at just those ages. This is a perfect fit. My administration will reform Head Start programs and aggressively emphasize early reading skills.

Head Start was originally intended as a literacy program, designed to close the achievement gap between rich and poor. It evolved into a day-care, health and nutrition program. And it has done good work, not only helping poor children, but also employing some of their parents as teachers and aides. Yet at $4.4 billion a year, it could be accomplishing so much more.Last year, Washington set some new goals for this program. Now we need a president to strongly implement them. My administration will move Head Start out of the Department of Health and Human Services and over to the Department of Education. Head Start will be an education program. It will fund only those local centers that emphasize the first steps toward reading and school-readiness. We will provide them with the basic research and material on early childhood education. And each time a Head Start contract is up for renewal, we will subject that site to an independent evaluation - to make sure they are successfully putting our children on the track to learning and literacy. If not, the operation of a Head Start site will be put up for competitive bidding - allowing someone, including churches and synagogues and community groups, to serve our children better. These children deserve the opportunities found in many private preschools, with trained teachers and high expectations. And all this will be done without sacrificing Head Start's important social and medical services.

The third reform concerns Title I - at $7.7 billion, the federal government's largest educational commitment to poor children. I respect that commitment, and will honor it. But I do not respect poor results with public money. In my administration, federal money will no longer flow to failure. Public funds must be spent on things that work.

My plan will make sure that every school getting Title I funds tests its disadvantaged students on the academic basics every year.

The state, not the federal government, will choose and administer those tests. If the scores are improving - making progress toward the state standard - a school will be rewarded with a grant and special recognition. If the disadvantaged children in a school are not making progress, the school will be warned that it is failing. It will be given time to adjust, to reform, to change. But if, at the end of three years, there is still no progress, its Title I funds will be divided up, matched by other federal education money given to the state, and made directly available to parents - coming to about $1,500 per year. This money can then be used by students for tutoring, for a charter school, for a working public school in a different district, for a private school - for whatever parents choose. For whatever offers hope.

States that want to pursue this kind of reform immediately will be free to do so. But eventually, in every case where a school does not teach and will not change, the status quo must be challenged.

The goal here is to strengthen public schools by expecting performance - to increase the number of schools where children are likely to learn. But if a school, with ample time to change, continues to fail, there must be some final point of accountability. Some moment of truth. In the best case, these schools will rise to the challenge and regain the confidence of parents. In the worst case, we will offer scholarships to America's neediest children, allowing them to get the emergency help they should have. In any case, the federal government will no longer pay schools to cheat poor children.

The enormous frustration with public education in America leads to two temptations. One is to dictate local policies from Washington. But this is an approach that has been discredited by 30 years of failure. Our schools do not need more bureaucratic oversight, they need the pressure to perform and the freedom to change. Education, it's been said, is not the filling of a pail, it is the lighting of a fire. We need that spirit today, and no master plan of government can light it.

But there is another temptation - to give up on public education entirely. To talk only of ending agencies or slashing programs. But this approach is too limited. One sixth of the American population is in public schools. The content of their education will determine the character of our country. Will America be prepared for the new economy? Will we have the informed citizens that self-government requires?

At their best, America's public schools have been a source of shared ideals. They gave millions of immigrants a start in life and a dream to follow. They were united by a golden thread of principle: that everyone, if given a chance, could rise in the world and contribute to their country. In all its simplicity, that is still the mission and mandate of public education in America.

A president does not bear responsibility for every policy in every school in every district. But every president must be the keeper of our common ideals. A president speaks for everyone. Not just for schools and those who run them. Not for one interest or ethnic group over another. Not for one class above the rest. A president - and sometimes only a president - can speak for the common good.

Our common good is found in our common schools. And we must make those schools worthy of all our children. Whatever their background, their cause is our cause, and it must not be lost.

<u>Position Paper</u>
Education: No Child Left Behind

"More and more, we are divided into two nations, separate and unequal. One that reads and one that can't. One that dreams and one that doesn't...All children can learn, and no child should be left behind."

Governor George W. Bush

EXECUTIVE SUMMARY

Governor Bush believes all children can learn, and no child should be left behind. That is why he considers it a scandal that the educational achievement gap between rich and poor, Anglo and minority, is not only wide, but in key areas such as reading, is wider than it was in 1992.

As President, Governor Bush will commit his administration to closing the achievement gap, as he is doing in Texas. During each of his years as Governor, all ethnic groups in Texas - in all grades - have advanced in reading and math. Indeed, according to the National Education Goals Panel, Texas is one of two states that has made the greatest progress in education in recent years.

While our children's education remains the primary concern of states, communities, and parents, Governor Bush believes the federal government can - and must - help close the achievement gap through three key reforms:

To Ensure that Federal Education Programs Produce Results, Governor Bush will:

- Require federally funded programs to boost student achievement, or be replaced by programs that succeed in reducing the achievement gap.

- Reform the Office of Education Research and Improvement so that it operates independently and scientifically, and empowers states with research on how to teach children most effectively.

To Make Education the Top Priority of Head Start, Governor Bush will:

- Move Head Start to the Education Department and make school readiness - instruction of pre-reading and numeracy skills - its top priority.

- Require Head Start programs to adopt a proven core curriculum.

- Award Head Start contracts on a competitive basis to spur improvements.

To Ensure that Federal Funds Underwrite Success Not Failure, Governor Bush will:

- Require states to improve academic performance for federally benefited students in return for federal funding and unprecedented flexibility.

- Award "Achievement in Education" bonus funds to states and schools that are closing the achievement gap.

- Require states to offer parents of Title I students stuck in persistently failing schools the option of using their federal education dollars to participate in another school or program of their choice.

The National Achievement Gap Has Grown During the 1990s

Governor Bush is concerned that the educational achievement gap is not only wide, but in some cases, growing wider still:

- Disparity between ethnic group performance on the National Assessment of Education Progress (NAEP) has grown or remained substantial in most subjects. The NAEP is the only nationally representative continuing assessment of what America's students know in key subject areas.

- The achievement gap on NAEP math and reading exams has widened since 1990. The reading gap between African-American, Hispanic, and white students is larger today than it was in 1992.

- The Administration concedes 68 percent of fourth graders in the highest poverty schools could not read in 1998 at NAEP's "basic" level. In low-poverty schools, by contrast, more than three quarters of the children read at or above the basic level.

- In a 1998 report, the Citizens' Commission on Civil Rights criticized "the widespread propensity of school officials to maintain and tolerate a permanent underclass of low-achieving students who are disproportionately poor and minority."

Governor Bush believes that it is precisely among these disadvantaged children in struggling schools that educational failure exacts its highest price. He believes we owe these children the pride and promise of learning - and that the new "knowledge-based" economy demands it.

A Philosophy of Reform

In the last several years, a movement of parents and legislators, voters and educators, has resulted in an explosion of innovation in education. This movement is proving public education can be improved dramatically. Governor Bush believes that out of these efforts a philosophy of reform aimed at a culture of excellence is emerging, based upon these principles:

- **First,** schools must have clear, measurable goals. These goals should be focused on the acquisition of basic skills and essential knowledge.

- **Second,** there must be regular testing and measurement to ensure that the goals are met. Education is about results, and testing helps educators and parents judge whether the desired results are being achieved.

- **Third,** effective reform requires accountability. The only sure way to create a culture of excellence is to have incentives for success and consequences for failure.

- **Fourth,** accountability must be accompanied by local control. If schools are to be held to high standards, they must have the freedom to meet those standards as they think best.

- **Finally,** competition is an essential ingredient in raising standards and creating accountability. Only the pressure of competition - and the power of parental choice - can change the status quo.

The Federal Role in Education – Making Sure No Child is Left Behind

Governor Bush believes the federal government can - and must - play a key role in closing the achievement gap. In return for increased federal funds and unprecedented flexibility in using those funds, the states must be held accountable for improving the academic achievement of students who benefit from federal assistance. The federal government should offer incentives for success in narrowing the achievement gap, impose consequences for failure, and encourage competition to spur improvement. As President, Governor Bush will champion three key reforms designed to ensure no child is left behind.

Reform #1: Ensure that Federal Education Programs Produce Results

The federal government funds more than 760 different education programs. These programs produce a lot of paperwork: it is estimated that processing forms alone requires 25,000 full-time employees. What is not known is whether these programs produce results. Unfortunately, federal money too often funds faddish, rather than rigorous research, and too few federal programs are scientifically evaluated.

The Department of Education's Office of Educational Research and Improvement (OERI) is supposed to sponsor reliable research. But despite receiving $510 million annually, it has generally failed to fulfill its task of developing and disseminating successful teaching techniques.

OERI's largest sponsored research program is the ten regional education laboratories, funded at $50 million a year. Established in 1965, the labs were intended to help states discover and implement what works in education. Instead, they have undertaken research that is fragmented, faddish, and vulnerable to politicization. Two former Assistant Secretaries of OERI have written that the regional labs "undertake a mishmash of research, dissemination, and technical assistance activities, aimed mostly at state and local education agencies...the program as a whole has outlived whatever justification it once had."

Governor Bush believes solid research in education can identify the most effective means of teaching children and closing the achievement gap. For example, recent National Institutes of Health research has shown that phonics-based instruction is a necessary component of teaching children to read. Research on early learning must also be a priority so solid curricula and teaching strategies for use in Head Start and other pre-school settings can be developed.

Therefore, as President, Governor Bush will:

<u>Require that the Federal Investment in Education Demonstrate Results:</u> The

federal government will insist that every program it funds will boost student achievement, or else it will be replaced by other education programs that succeed in reducing the achievement gap.

Reform the Office of Education Research and Improvement: In order to generate valid research that will empower the states, districts, and educators with research-based programs that most effectively teach children, OERI will be overhauled to ensure that it operates independently and consistently with the standards of a science-based research center. The regional education laboratories, which have failed to meet their purpose of providing helpful research to states and educators, will be sunset and opened to competitive bid.

Reform #2: Return Head Start to its Original Purpose - Education

Effective early childhood education programs can have a tremendous bearing on the future academic success of our children. That is why Governor Bush believes that Head Start should be reformed, not scrapped.

Established in 1965, Head Start was intended as a program to close the achievement gap. Today, it is the largest federal early childhood development program, funded at $4.4 billion a year. It serves more than 840,000 low-income children, most of whom are three- and four-year-olds. It is administered through the Department of Health and Human Services (HHS), which contracts with local providers to run the programs.

However, while some local Head Start programs have produced cognitive gains for participating youngsters, there is no pervasive evidence of the educational effectiveness of Head Start as a whole. The largest evaluation of Head Start to date, an April 1997 GAO report summarizing the findings of nearly 600 Head Start studies, shows that after three decades, Head Start lacks consistent results in preparing children academically for school.

Thus, to reform Head Start, Governor Bush will:

Move Head Start to the Department of Education: To ensure that Head Start makes education a priority and focuses on building skills for school readiness, especially pre-reading and numeracy, the Department of Education, not HHS, will oversee the administration and evaluation of local Head Start programs.

Require Head Start Programs to Adopt a Proven Core Curriculum: The federal government will identify model curricula and effective methods of teaching pre-reading and school readiness. These research-based best practices will be made available to local Head Start programs so they can better prepare youngsters to enter school ready to learn.

Award Head Start Contracts on a Competitive Basis: New Head Start grants will be open to competition and awarded on a selective basis. Upon renewal of each existing Head Start contract, the program will be evaluated based on its effectiveness. If a program is found ineffective in teaching pre-reading and school readiness, its contract will be opened up for competitive bid.

Reform #3: Restructure Title I to Close the Achievement Gap

Title I was created in 1965 as the federal government's principal means of closing the achievement gap between the children of low-income families and their counterparts. It provides $7.7 billion annually to local school districts to supplement the education of 11 million low-income students. Nearly half of all public schools and 94 percent of all school districts now receive Title I money.

Little evidence exists that Title I has made any appreciable progress in closing the achievement gap. Two long-term studies mandated by Congress, "Sustaining Effects" in the late 1970's and "Prospects" in the early 1990's, concluded that after billions of dollars, Title I had achieved virtually no lasting gains in academic improvement. Even the most recent study, the "Longitudinal Evaluation of School Change and Performance," begun after the 1994 reform of Title I, reports disappointing results. The interim report, released to Congress in July of 1999, seems to suggest Title I students are growing academically at less than a year's progress for each year in school.

Governor Bush believes we must stop using federal money to fund failure by imposing quick and rigorous consequences for performance. Schools that produce results should be rewarded. But when a school fails - after being given an opportunity to change - its Title I funds should be given directly to parents to use for the educational program or school of their choice.

As President, Governor Bush will administer Title I to ensure that schools have both the pressure to perform and the freedom to succeed. Specifically, he will:

Focus Title I Funds on Earlier Grades: Students in K-12 will still be eligible for Title I, but Title I funds will focus on students in the elementary grades, where the achievement gap in reading and math skills begins.

Hold Schools Accountable for Performance of Title I Students: All states must annually assess Title I students in grades 3-8 in reading and math and report the results on a disaggregated basis. Each state that has not already done so must adopt its own standards of acceptable student performance and institute reforms that will move Title I students toward that standard through improved academic results, thus closing the achievement gap.

Establish an "Achievement in Education" Fund to Reward Success: States that make the greatest progress in closing the gap for economically disadvantaged students and schools within each state that make the greatest gains in moving Title I students toward the state-set standards will be rewarded significantly through an "Achievement in Education" bonus fund.

Give Low-Performing Schools Three Years to Reform: States will have three years to reform failing Title I schools by restructuring management, changing personnel, reallocating resources, taking over persistently low-performing schools or districts, transferring education dollars to the parents, and/or implementing a school choice system. If a state enacts private or public school choice, it should be able to offer parents of Title I students in failing schools a pro-rata share of Title I funds to help pay for these choice options.

Make Funds Portable After Three Years: If, after three years, state reforms have not worked and the combined academic results of Title I students enrolled in a school still do not demonstrate progress toward the state-set standard of acceptable performance, the state will be required to:

- Give Title I students in these schools the option (fully paid for) of transferring to a school that is closing the gap for such students; or

- Offer parents of these students portable funds, which can be used to obtain for their child an education at a school of their choice or supplemental education services. These funds (worth an average $1,500 per child) will consist of the student's pro rata share of Title I funds, provided by the Local Education Agency, and an equal amount provided by the state from its federal or state funds. Portability would be in effect for the period of time the child would have been enrolled in the failing school.

What Others Say

"...the most fundamental reform to public education... in a generation... tells parents the truth about their own child's education. No candidate for President has ever looked so thoroughly, and understood so fundamentally, what ails our schools."

Lynne Munson, American Enterprise Institute

"...wants education goals to be simple and clear... rather than trust federal intervention, Mr. Bush would rather empower parents with scholarships."

Editorial, <u>The Washington Post</u>, 9/5/99

"Texas school children have been having rising test scores under George W. Bush."

Thomas Sowell, <u>Austin-American Statesman</u>, 9/11/99

"I laud him on making education a focus and turning up the flame on school reform."

Duren Cheek, <u>The Tennessean</u>, 9/3/99

"The governor's easy command of specifics on the education topic will come as no surprise to his fellow Texans. We know George W. Bush's record. We have felt the force of his intense personal commitment."

Charles Miller, <u>The Houston Chronicle</u>, 9/5/99

"...reform plan is impressive...A Real Education President."

Checker Finn, Jr., <u>The Weekly Standard</u>, 9/20/99

"Mr. Bush has a plan...a good one, to use the federal government affirmatively, by saying if your schools are failing, some of our money will go in voucher form to the parents of those schools."

George Will, ABC, "This Week," 9/5/99

2

Education:
A Culture of Achievement

Manhattan Institute Luncheon

October 5, 1999

Last month in California, I talked about disadvantaged children in troubled schools. I argued that the diminished hopes of our current system are sad and serious – the soft bigotry of low expectations.

And I set out a simple principle: Federal funds will no longer flow to failure. Schools that do not teach and will not change must have some final point of accountability. A moment of truth, when their Title I funds are divided up and given to parents, for tutoring or a charter school or some other hopeful option. In the best case, schools that are failing will rise to the challenge and regain the confidence of parents. In the worst case, we will offer scholarships to America's neediest children.

In any case, the federal government will no longer pay schools to cheat poor children.

But this is the beginning of our challenge, not its end. The final object of education reform is not just to shun mediocrity; it is to seek excellence. It is not just to avoid failure; it is to encourage achievement.

Our nation has a moral duty to ensure that no child is left behind.

And we also, at this moment, have a great national opportunity – to ensure that every child, in every public school, is challenged by high standards that meet the high hopes of parents. To build a culture of achievement that matches the optimism and aspirations of our country.

Not long ago, this would have seemed incredible. Our education debates were captured by a deep pessimism.

For decades, waves of reform were quickly revealed as passing fads, with little lasting result. For decades, funding rose while performance stagnated. Most parents, except in some urban districts, have not seen the collapse of education. They have seen a slow slide of expectations and standards. Schools where poor spelling is called "creative." Where math is "fuzzy" and grammar is optional. Where grade inflation is the norm.

Schools where spelling bees are canceled for being too competitive and selecting a single valedictorian is considered too exclusive. Where advancing from one grade to the next is unconnected to advancing skills. Schools where, as in <u>Alice in Wonderland,</u> "Everyone has won, and all must have prizes."

We are left with a nagging sense of lost potential. A sense of what could be, but is not.

It led the late Albert Shanker, of the American Federation of Teachers, to conclude: "Very few American pupils are performing anywhere near where they could be performing."

This cuts against the grain of American character. Most parents know that the self-esteem of children is not built by low standards, it is built by real accomplishments. Most parents know that good character is tied to an ethic of study and hard work and merit – and that setbacks are as much a part of learning as awards.

Most Americans know that a healthy democracy must be committed both to equality and to excellence.

Until a few years ago, the debates of politics seemed irrelevant to these concerns. Democrats and Republicans argued mainly about funding and procedures – about dollars and devolution. Few talked of standards or accountability or of excellence for all our children.

But all this is beginning to change. In state after state, we are seeing a profound shift of priorities. An "age of accountability" is starting to replace an era of low expectations. And there is a growing conviction and confidence that the problems of public education are not an endless road or a hopeless maze.

The principles of this movement are similar from New York to Florida, from Massachusetts to Michigan. Raise the bar of standards.

Give schools the flexibility to meet them. Measure progress. Insist on results. Blow the whistle on failure. Provide parents with options to increase their influence. And don't give up on anyone.

There are now countless examples of public schools transformed by great expectations. Places like Earhart Elementary in Chicago, where students are expected to compose essays by the second grade.

Where these young children participate in a Junior Great Books program, and sixth graders are reading <u>To Kill a Mockingbird</u>. The principal explains, "All our children are expected to work above grade level and learn for the sake of learning... We instill a desire to overachieve. Give us an average child and we'll make him an overachiever."

This is a public school, and not a wealthy one. And it proves what is possible.

No one in Texas now doubts that public schools can improve. We are witnessing the promise of high standards and accountability. We require that every child read by the third grade, without exception or excuse. Every year, we test students on the academic basics. We disclose those results by school. We encourage the diversity and creativity of charters. We give local schools and districts the freedom to chart their own path to excellence.

I certainly don't claim credit for all these changes. But my state is proud of what we have accomplished together. Last week, the federal Department of Education announced that Texas eighth graders have some of the best writing skills in the country. In 1994, there were 67 schools in Texas rated "exemplary" according to our tests. This year, there are 1,120. We are proud, but we are not content. Now that we are meeting our current standards, I am insisting that we elevate those standards.

Now that we are clearing the bar, we are going to raise the bar – because we have set our sights on excellence.

At the beginning of the 1990s, so many of our nation's problems, from education to crime to welfare, seemed intractable – beyond our control. But something unexpected happened on the way to cultural decline. Problems that seemed inevitable proved to be reversible. They gave way to an optimistic, governing conservatism.

Here in New York, Mayor Giuliani brought order and civility back to the streets – cutting crime rates by 50 percent. In Wisconsin, Governor Tommy Thompson proved that welfare dependence could be reversed – reducing his rolls by 91 percent. Innovative mayors and governors followed their lead – cutting national welfare rolls by nearly half since 1994, and reducing the murder rate to the lowest point since 1967.

Now education reform is gaining a critical mass of results.

In the process, conservatism has become the creed of hope. The creed of aggressive, persistent reform. The creed of social progress.

Too often, on social issues, my party has painted an image of America slouching toward Gomorrah. Of course there are challenges to the character and compassion of our nation – too many broken homes and broken lives.

But many of our problems – particularly education, crime and welfare dependence – are yielding to good sense and strength and idealism. In states and cities around the country, we are making, not just points and pledges, but progress. We are demonstrating the genius for self-renewal at the heart of the American experiment.

Too often, my party has focused on the national economy, to the exclusion of all else – speaking a sterile language of rates and numbers, of CBO this and GNP that.

Of course we want growth and vigor in our economy. But there are human problems that persist in the shadow of affluence. And the strongest argument for conservative ideals – for responsibility and accountability and the virtues of our tradition – is that they lead to greater justice, less suffering, more opportunity.

Too often, my party has confused the need for limited government with a disdain for government itself.

But this is not an option for conservatives. At the constitutional Convention in 1787, Benjamin Franklin argued that the strength of our nation depends "on the general opinion of the goodness of government." Our Founders rejected cynicism, and cultivated a noble love of country. That love is undermined by sprawling, arrogant, aimless government. It is restored by focused and effective and energetic government.

And that should be our goal: A limited government, respected for doing a few things and doing them well.

This is an approach with echoes in our history. Echoes of Lincoln and emancipation and the Homestead Act and land-grant colleges. Echoes of Theodore Roosevelt and national parks and the Panama Canal. Echoes of Reagan and a confrontation with communism that sought victory, not stalemate.

What are the issues that challenge us, that summon us, in our time? Surely one of them must be excellence in education. Surely one of them must be to rekindle the spirit of learning and ambition in our common schools. And one of our great opportunities and urgent duties is to remake the federal role.

Even as many states embrace education reform, the federal

31

government is mired in bureaucracy and mediocrity.

It is an obstacle, not an ally. Education bills are often rituals of symbolic spending without real accountability – like pumping gas into a flooded engine. For decades, fashionable ideas have been turned into programs, with little knowledge of their benefits for students and teachers. And even the obvious failures seldom disappear.

This is a perfect example of government that is big – and weak. Of government that is grasping – and impotent.

Let me share an example. The Department of Education recently streamlined the grant application process for states. The old procedure involved 487 different steps, taking an average of 26 weeks. So, a few years ago, the best minds of the administration got together and "reinvented" the grant process. Now it takes a mere 216 steps, and the wait is 20 weeks.

If this is reinventing government, it makes you wonder how this administration was ever skilled enough and efficient enough to create the Internet. I don't want to tinker with the machinery of the federal role in education. I want to redefine that role entirely.

I strongly believe in local control of schools and curriculum. I have consistently placed my faith in states and schools and parents and teachers – and that faith, in Texas, has been rewarded.

I also believe a president should define and defend the unifying ideals of our nation – including the quality of our common schools. He must lead, without controlling. He must set high goals – without being high-handed. The inertia of our education bureaucracy is a national problem, requiring a national response. Sometimes inaction is not restraint – it is complicity. Sometimes it takes the use of executive power to empower others.

Effective education reform requires both pressure from above and competition from below – a demand for high standards and measurement at the top, given momentum and urgency by expanded options for parents and students. So, as president, here is what

I'll do. First, I will fundamentally change the relationship of the states and federal government in education. Now we have a system of excessive regulation and no standards. In my administration, we will have minimal regulation and high standards.

Second, I will promote more choices for parents in the education of their children. In the end, it is parents, armed with information and options, who turn the theory of reform into the reality of excellence.

All reform begins with freedom and local control. It unleashes creativity. It permits those closest to children to exercise their judgment. And it also removes the excuse for failure. Only those with the ability to change can be held to account.

But local control has seldom been a priority in Washington. In 1965, when President Johnson signed the very first Elementary and Secondary Education Act, not one school board trustee, from anywhere in the country, was invited to the ceremony. Local officials were viewed as the enemy. And that attitude has lingered too long.

As president, I will begin by taking most of the 60 different categories of federal education grants and paring them down to five: improving achievement among disadvantaged children; promoting fluency in English; training and recruiting teachers; encouraging character and school safety; and promoting innovation and parental choice. Within these divisions, states will have maximum flexibility to determine their priorities.

They will only be asked to certify that their funds are being used for the specific purposes intended – and the federal red tape ends there.

This will spread authority to levels of government that people can touch. And it will reduce paperwork – allowing schools to spend less on filing forms and more on what matters: teachers' salaries and children themselves.

In return, we will ask that every state have a real accountability system – meaning that they test every child, every year, in grades three through eight, on the basics of reading and math; broadly disclose those results by school, including on the Internet; and have clear consequences for success and failure. States will pick their own tests, and the federal government will share the costs of administering them.

States can choose tests off-the-shelf, like Arizona; adapt tests like California; or contract for new tests like Texas. Over time, if a state's results are improving, it will be rewarded with extra money – a total of $500 million in awards over five years. If scores are stagnant or dropping, the administrative portion of their federal funding – about 5 percent – will be diverted to a fund for charter schools.

We will praise and reward success – and shine a spotlight of shame on failure.

What I am proposing today is a fresh start for the federal role in education. A pact of principle. Freedom in exchange for achievement. Latitude in return for results. Local control with one national goal: excellence for every child.

I am opposed to national tests, written by the federal government.

If Washington can control the content of tests, it can dictate the content of state curricula – a role our central government should not play.

But measurement at the state level is essential. Without testing, reform is a journey without a compass. Without testing, teachers and administrators cannot adjust their methods to meet high goals. Without testing, standards are little more than scraps of paper.

Without testing, true competition is impossible. Without testing, parents are left in the dark.

In fact, the greatest benefit of testing – with the power to transform a school or a system – is the information it gives to parents. They will know – not just by rumor or reputation, but by hard numbers – which schools are succeeding and which are not.

Given that information, more parents will be pulled into activism – becoming participants, not spectators, in the education of their children. Armed with that information, parents will have the leverage to force reform.

Information is essential. But reform also requires options. Monopolies seldom change on their own – no matter how good the intentions of those who lead them. Competition is required to jolt a bureaucracy out of its lethargy.

So my second goal for the federal role of education is to increase the options and influence of parents.

The reform of Title I I've proposed would begin this process. We will give parents with children in failing schools – schools where the test scores of Title I children show no improvement over three years – the resources to seek more hopeful options. This will amount to a scholarship of about $1,500 a year.

And parents can use those funds for tutoring or tuition – for anything that gives their children a fighting chance at learning. The theory is simple. Public funds must be spent on things that work – on helping children, not sustaining failed schools that refuse to change.

The response to this plan has been deeply encouraging. Yet some politicians have gone to low performing schools and claimed my plan would undermine them.

Think a moment about what that means. It means visiting a school and saying, in essence, "You are hopeless. Not only can't you achieve, you can't even improve." That is not a defense of public education, it is a surrender to despair. That is not liberalism, it is pessimism. It is accepting and excusing an educational apartheid in our country – segregating poor children into a world without the hope of change.

Everyone, in both parties, seems to agree with accountability in theory. But what could accountability possibly mean if children

35

attend schools for 12 years without learning to read or write? Accountability without consequences is empty – the hollow shell of reform. And all our children deserve better.

In our education reform plan, we will give states more flexibility to use federal funds, at their option, for choice programs – including private school choice.

In some neighborhoods, these new options are the first sign of hope, of real change, that parents have seen for a generation.

But not everyone wants or needs private school choice. Many parents in America want more choices, higher standards and more influence *within* their public schools. This is the great promise of charter schools – the path that New York is now beginning. And this, in great part, is a tribute to the Manhattan Institute.

If charters are properly done – free to hire their own teachers, adopt their own curriculum, set their own operating rules and high standards – they will change the face of American education. Public schools – without bureaucracy. Public schools – controlled by parents. Public schools – held to the highest goals. Public schools – as we imagined they could be.

For parents, they are schools on a human scale, where their voice is heard and heeded. For students, they are more like a family than a factory – a place where it is harder to get lost. For teachers, who often help found charter schools, they are a chance to teach as they've always wanted. Says one charter school teacher in Boston: "We don't have to wait to make changes. We don't have to wait for the district to decide that what we are doing is within the rules...So we can really put the interests of the kids first."

This morning I visited the new Sisulu Children's Academy in Harlem – New York's first charter school. In an area where only a quarter of children can read at or above grade level, Sisulu Academy offers a core curriculum of reading, math, science and history. There will be an extended school day, and the kids will also learn computer skills, art, music and dance. And there is a waiting list of 100 children.

This is a new approach – even a new definition of public education. These schools are public because they are publicly funded and publicly accountable for results. The vision of parents and teachers and principals determines the rest. Money follows the child. The units of delivery get smaller and more personal. Some charters go back to basics...some attract the gifted...some emphasize the arts.

It is a reform movement that welcomes diversity, but demands excellence. And this is the essence of real reform.

Charter schools benefit the children within them – as well as the public school students beyond them. The evidence shows that competition often strengthens all the schools in a district. In Arizona, in places where charters have arrived – teaching phonics and extending hours and involving parents – suddenly many traditional public schools are following suit.

The greatest problem facing charter schools is practical – the cost of building them. Unlike regular public schools, they receive no capital funds. And the typical charter costs about $1.5 million to construct. Some are forced to start in vacant hotel rooms or strip malls.

As president, I want to fan the spark of charter schools into a flame. My administration will establish a Charter School Homestead Fund, to help finance these start-up costs.

We will provide capital to education entrepreneurs – planting new schools on the frontiers of reform. This fund will support $3 billion in loan guarantees in my first two years in office – enough to seed 2,000 schools. Enough to double the existing number.

This will be a direct challenge to the status quo in public education – in a way that both changes it and strengthens it. With charters, someone cares enough to say, "I'm dissatisfied."

Someone is bold enough to say, "I can do better." And all our schools will aim higher if we reward that kind of courage and vision.

And we will do one thing more for parents. We will expand Education Savings Accounts to cover education expenses in grades K through 12, allowing parents or grandparents to contribute up to $5,000 dollars per year, per student. Those funds can be withdrawn tax-free for tuition payments, or books, or tutoring or transportation – whatever students need most.

Often this nation sets out to reform education for all the wrong reasons – or at least for incomplete ones. Because the Soviets launch Sputnik. Or because children in Singapore have high test scores. Or because our new economy demands computer operators.

But when parents hope for their children, they hope with nobler goals. Yes, we want them to have the basic skills of life. But life is more than a race for riches.

A good education leads to intellectual self-confidence, and ambition and a quickened imagination. It helps us, not just to live, but to live well.

And this private good has public consequences. In his first address to Congress, President Washington called education "the surest basis of public happiness." America's founders believed that self-government requires a certain kind of citizen.

Schooled to think clearly and critically, and to know America's civic ideals. Freed, by learning, to rise, by merit. Education is the way a democratic culture reproduces itself through time.

This is the reason a conservative should be passionate about education reform – the reason a conservative should fight strongly and care deeply. Our common schools carry a great burden for the common good. And they must be more than schools of last resort.

Every child must have a quality education – not just in islands of excellence. Because we are a single nation with a shared future. Because, as Lincoln said, we are "brothers of a common country."

Position Paper
Education: A Culture of Achievement

"The final object of education reform is not just to shun mediocrity; it is to seek excellence. It is not just to avoid failure; it is to reward achievement. Our nation has a moral duty to ensure no child is left behind. And we also, at this moment, have a great national opportunity – to ensure that every child, in every public school, is challenged by high standards that meet the high hopes of parents. To build a culture of achievement that matches the optimism and aspirations of our country."

Governor George W. Bush

EXECUTIVE SUMMARY

Governor Bush believes America must be committed to both equality and excellence in education. In addition to closing the achievement gap between rich and poor students, we must raise standards of excellence for <u>all</u> students. This requires pressure from above for high standards, and competition from below to provide parents and students with information and options. Thus, as President, Governor Bush will:

Redefine the relationship between the states and the federal government, granting freedom from regulation in exchange for results. Specifically, he will:

- Free states from regulation by consolidating most of the 60 elementary and secondary education programs into 5 flexible categories: improving achievement of disadvantaged children, promoting fluency in English, training and recruiting teachers, encouraging character and school safety, and promoting innovation and informed parental choice.

- Offer states the option to become "charter" states, providing them with even more flexibility in return for meeting rigorous performance standards.

- Require all states to establish an accountability system in which they test every child, every year, in grades 3 through 8 on reading and math. States will be free to choose their own tests, and the federal government will equally share the cost.

- Pay for states to administer an annual National Assessment of Educational Progress (NAEP) sample exam, or its equivalent, in reading and math.

- Establish a $500 million fund to reward states that improve student performance, and commit to withdraw the administrative portion of federal funding – about 5 percent – from states that permit student performance to stagnate or decline.

Promote competition to increase the options and influence of parents. Specifically, he will:

- Require school-by-school report cards to be published on the Internet and elsewhere.

- Establish a Charter School Homestead Fund to provide $3 billion of loan guarantees to help establish or improve 2,000 charter schools in two years.

- Expand Education Savings Accounts by allowing parents to increase their annual contributions from $500 per student to $5,000, and withdraw funds tax free to pay for education expenses from kindergarten to college.

Redefining the Federal Role in Education

Determined parents, educators, and legislators across America have embraced education reform. Too often, however, these reformers are finding that the heavy hand of federal bureaucracy is hindering their efforts.

Federal education dollars are spread over too many programs – and cost too much to administer. The paperwork involved in tracking and accounting for federal dollars drains resources from schools that would be better spent on teachers' salaries and students. In some states, an estimated 50 percent of paperwork done by local schools is spent administering federal education programs, even though federal funds account for only 7 percent of total spending. According to a 1998 study by the U.S. Department of Education, only 85 cents out of every federal education dollar actually reaches the school district, and even less reaches the classroom.

But federal red tape is not the only problem reformers face. Not only does the federal system currently fail to provide states with the flexibility they need to improve their schools, the system also fails to demand academic results:

- A 1997 GAO report on federal education funding stated that "federally funded programs have historically placed a low priority on results and accountability."

- A 1998 report by the U.S. House Subcommittee on Education found that "it has been years since many [federal education] programs have been evaluated, and often those reviews are more concerned with process – accounting for numbers of participants and educators, not whether the children are actually better off."

Governor Bush believes that the "era of low expectations" must now be replaced with an "age of accountability." Effective school reform requires pressure from above to establish high standards, and competition from below to expand information and options for parents and students. Thus, as President, to promote a culture of excellence in the nation's schools, Governor Bush will:

- Redefine the relationship between the states and the federal government, offering states unprecedented freedom from regulation in exchange for measurable achievement; and

- Increase the options and influence of parents by providing information on school performance and promoting competition.

Goal #1: A New Federal-State Education Pact – Freedom in Exchange for Results

Governor Bush believes that to reform education it is necessary to redefine the relationship between the states and the federal government. Therefore, he is proposing a new federal-state pact offering freedom from regulation and bureaucratic red tape, in exchange for achievement.

41

A. Freedom from Regulation

The Elementary and Secondary Education Act (ESEA), established in 1965, is the largest source of federal funding for K-12 education. It provides nearly $14 billion annually through more than 60 different programs designated under 13 different Titles. The largest portion of these funds is contained in Title I, an $8 billion program aimed at assisting disadvantaged children. Other ESEA programs address issues ranging from teacher training to teen drug use to funding for arts in education.

The proliferation of ESEA programs has generated a corresponding increase in regulation and red tape. As a result, hearings held by the House Education and Workforce Committee in 1997 revealed that the U.S. government spends almost twice as much on administering education programs as other industrialized countries.

The complexity of the ESEA system also imposes higher costs on the states. In the state of Georgia, for example, it takes 4.5 times as many people to administer a federal education dollar as it does to administer a state education dollar.

As President, Governor Bush will free the states from the regulation, red tape, and high costs of administering ESEA funds. Specifically, Governor Bush will:

<u>Consolidate and Simplify ESEA Funding</u>: The current categorical system of 60 separate programs will be replaced with five flexible categories, representing broad education goals:

- Improving the Academic Performance of Disadvantaged Students.

- Moving Limited English Proficient (LEP) Students to English Fluency.

- Preparing, Training and Recruiting Qualified Teachers.

- Creating a Safe Culture for Learning.

- Promoting Informed Parental Choice and Research-based Innovative Practices.

A few specific programs, such as Impact Aid, which is granted to districts affected by military bases and other federal activities, will remain unchanged. Administrative funds will be separated and provided in one lump sum.

<u>Eliminate Restrictions and Red Tape</u>: Within the five broad categories, states will have freedom to determine priorities and to assign responsibility for

administering the funds within state government, so long as they certify that the funds are being spent for the intended purposes.

Offer States the Option to Become "Charter" States: States will have the option of entering into a charter agreement with the federal government, whereby they would commit to meet especially high levels of academic achievement for all students, particularly disadvantaged ones, in exchange for further consolidation of their federal education funding – and further flexibility in spending. The same contract option will also be made available to individual districts.

B. Accountability

In return for this increased freedom from regulation, Governor Bush will ask that every state implement an accountability system, involving high standards and regular performance measurement.

Many states have set education standards, but often they are too low to ensure excellence. In 1998, the Fordham Foundation appraised state standards in English, history, geography, mathematics, and science. Independent reviewers assigned a letter grade – A, B, C, D, or F – to each state, based on the clarity, rigor and effectiveness of the state standards. The results showed most state standards must be improved before they will guarantee excellence. When assigned composite grades based on the average grades of all its standards, no state earned an "A" average; only three earned "B" averages; and nine flunked. The national cumulative GPA was a "D +."

Governor Bush believes that not only should high standards be set, they must be accompanied by performance measurement. Testing makes standards meaningful, promotes competition, and empowers parents and teachers to seek change. Unfortunately, while many states test some students, fewer than 12 states test all students in consecutive grades, every year.

As President, in exchange for giving states unprecedented freedom in spending federal funds, Governor Bush will:

Require States to Set Up Their Own Accountability Systems: All states receiving federal education assistance will be required to establish within three years an accountability system with the goal of achieving and demonstrating academic improvement. Each state will be free to set its own standards and craft its own system free of federal control, so long as those systems contain certain minimum elements:

• High standards in core subjects: math, English, science, and history.

43

- Annual assessment of all students in at least grades 3-8 in reading and math. States will be free to choose their own tests, and the federal government will share equally in the cost of administering them. Any student exemptions from testing should be based upon a limited and consistently applied standard.

- A commitment to reward school success and impose consequences for failure. States' responses to achievement results could include an array of actions, including honors and/or rewards; restructured management; personnel changes; takeover of persistently low-performing schools and districts; and even the transfer of education dollars to the parent and implementation of a choice system.

Ask States to Participate in Annual NAEP Exams: As part of the new federal-state education pact, the federal government will pay for states to participate in an annual National Assessment of Educational Progress (NAEP) sample exam, or its equivalent, for students in grades 4 and 8 in reading and math. All states receiving federal education assistance must participate in the sample exam, which can be done reliably with sample sizes of no more than 1,700 to 2,600 students per state. If a state would prefer to use another test in lieu of the NAEP and can show that its results can be equated with those of NAEP, the state can, at its own expense, use or continue using such a test.

Ensure an Independent NAEP: To insulate NAEP from political influence, the office that administers NAEP and the bipartisan board that sets policy for it, will be made independent of the Department of Education.

C. Consequences for Success and Failure

Governor Bush believes that accountability must be accompanied by consequences. As President, to ensure that success in achieving high standards is rewarded, while stagnating or declining performance is not tolerated, Governor Bush will:

Reward States that Demonstrate Academic Improvement: An "Achievement in Education" fund will be created to reward states that demonstrate substantial and valid progress on the state assessments, as verified by NAEP. A total of $500 million will be made available to be awarded over five years. Rewards will be based upon achievement of one or more of the following goals, with the size of the reward increasing with the number of goals achieved:

- closing the achievement gap, by raising the achievement of disadvantaged students.

- Increasing overall student performance, by raising the achievement of all students.

- Increasing opportunities for advanced academic achievement, by increasing, for example, the number of students who are deemed proficient on NAEP, raising SAT/ACT scores, and increasing the number of students who take and pass Advanced Placement and International Baccalaureate exams.

Impose Consequences on States that Fail to Demonstrate Results: States that fail to demonstrate results in academic achievement over the course of five years, will have the administrative portion of their federal funding – roughly 5 percent of the total – withdrawn and re-directed into the charter school grant fund.

Goal #2: Empower Parents by Promoting Competition

Governor Bush believes that increased competition is an essential ingredient in raising education standards. Ultimately, only the pressure of accountability and competition – combined with the power of parental choice – can change the status quo. Promoting effective competition will require parents to have information, options, and resources.

A. Information

Governor Bush believes that parents are the most important enforcers of accountability in education. But parents must be armed with more information to determine whether quality education is taking place. Unfortunately, too few parents have access to adequate information about their schools. A 1999 Education Week survey found that 76 percent of parents thought widely publicized ratings on such measures as test scores and graduation rates motivate public school teachers to work harder to improve schools' performance. Yet, only 39 percent of parents in the survey said that they had ever seen a school-by-school report card in their community. Indeed, currently, only 36 states provide parents with school-by-school report cards.

Governor Bush believes that information empowers parents, providing them with the leverage to press for change and a reason to become participants in the education of their children. As President, to arm parents with information, Governor Bush will:

- Require School-by-School Report Cards: States will be asked to provide school-by-school report cards, publicizing assessment and testing results, particularly in reading and math. The results should be disaggregated by race, gender, poverty, and English proficiency, and should be published widely, including on the Internet.

B. Charter Schools and Parental Choice

Information alone, however, is not enough to empower parents and spur competition. There must be viable options, as well. While vouchers for private schools represent one such option, most parents want more choices, higher standards and more influence within their public schools. That is the promise of the charter school movement. In charter schools, freedom and accountability combine with parental choice to create a culture of achievement.

Charter schools are independent public schools that are formed by teachers, community leaders, parents or others with a desire to break free of the bureaucracy and regulatory red tape that characterize too many of today's public school systems. Attendance at charter schools is free: funds that would otherwise be allocated to a child at his or her regular public school follow the child to the charter school.

Unlike traditional public schools, charter schools are held to the highest level of accountability – consumer demand. If charter schools fail to meet the expectations of parents and teachers, they will be unable to attract students and, as a result, their charters will be revoked.

The demand for charter schools is great. According to the Department of Education, the number of charter schools grew by more than 50 percent in 1998. Just seven years ago, there was only one charter school in existence. Today, 36 states and the District of Columbia have charter school laws, and there are over 350,000 students attending nearly 1,700 charter schools. Seven out of every ten charter schools have a waiting list of students.

According to the Pioneer Institute and the Department of Education, a lack of readily available start-up funding is the most significant barrier faced by charter school organizers. While the typical charter school receives 50 to 100 percent of the average funding per student allocated by the local school district to school <u>operations</u>, most receive no <u>capital</u> funds. The Department of Education offered $100 million in grants to charter schools in 1999, but those grants may be used only for equipment and teacher training, not to acquire, lease, or renovate a facility.

To encourage the growth of charter schools and spur competition, Governor Bush will:

<u>Create a "Charter School Homestead Fund</u>:" The fund will support $3 billion in loan guarantees to private lenders. The goal of the fund will be to upgrade or establish 2,000 charter schools – potentially doubling the number now in existence – within the first two years of Governor Bush's administration:

- The loan guarantees will be made available to lenders who agree to finance charter school start-up or improvement costs, including the acquisition, lease and/or renovation of a facility, teacher training, and the purchase of equipment and instructional material.

- To leverage private equity, the fund will provide guarantees ranging from 75 to 100 percent, depending upon the amount of private equity the organizers raise (the greater the equity, the higher the guarantee).

- Priority will be given to schools in states with charter laws that promote high standards and accountability, allow parental involvement, permit principals to select and terminate teachers, and reward teachers on performance.

- The existing grant program will be maintained and administered in coordination with the loan guarantees.

<u>Allow Federal Funds to Be Used for Choice in Education</u>: The consolidation of federal ESEA funds into a handful of flexible categories will allow states and districts to use these funds to expand educational options for parents, including private school choice programs.

C. Education Savings Accounts

Information on school performance, and options such as charter schools, will stimulate competition. Yet, many parents still need additional resources to deal with the specific needs of their children. Whether their children attend public, private, religious, charter, or home schools, parents need funds to pay fees, buy books and supplies, cover transportation costs, support after-school programs, and pay for tutoring and special needs.

In principle, education savings accounts could empower parents, allowing parent-directed dollars to be applied to specific problems. However, the current education savings accounts – which permit parents to contribute $500 annually and to withdraw those dollars tax free – can only be used to pay for college and other higher education expenses.

Unfortunately, President Clinton vetoed the Taxpayer Refund and Relief Act of 1999, which would have expanded the existing savings accounts by increasing the maximum annual contribution from $500 to $2,000, and by allowing the accounts to be used for expenses associated with K-12 education.

Thus, to empower parents with additional education resources, as President, Governor Bush will:

Expand Education Savings Accounts: Allow families or individuals with incomes up to $150,000 (or single earners with annual incomes up to $95,000) to contribute up to $5,000 annually per child into education savings accounts. Parents will be permitted to withdraw funds tax free (i.e., without being taxed on any gain or interest earned) to use for education-related purposes – from kindergarten to college and beyond – in public, private, religious, or home schools.

What Others Say

"Governor Bush's speech on education reform was serious, thoughtful and substantively impressive. The things Governor Bush advocates – high standards, testing, accountability, and choice – are precisely what is needed to help improve American education. Governor Bush is an eloquent advocate of fundamental education reform – and he has an impressive record of achievement on the issue."

Dr. Bill Bennett,
Former U.S. Secretary of Education

"Since 1995, when George W. Bush became governor, public school test scores have increased across the board for every ethnic group in every subject at every grade level.

Bush deserves much of the credit… he pushed for system deregulation and expansion of the options available to families…He set a limited number of clear goals, beginning with the goal that all children learn to read."

Editorial, Houston Chronicle, 9/5/99

"So indeed, maybe this is the time when we will have a true education President, George Walker Bush."

Floyd Flake, Former U.S. Representative (D-NY-6)

"Of all the candidates I've seen in the past twenty years, [Governor Bush] probably is one who offers the most comprehensive education plan very early in the campaign… at the end of the day having a president who embodies these values and talks about them will make more difference than any policy you put in place."

Nina Shokraii Rees, The Heritage Foundation

"Provides states much greater flexibility… strengthen(s)…accountability."

Ron Brownstein, LA Times, 10/6/99

3

Education:
The True Goal of Education

Northern White Mountain Chamber of Commerce

November 2, 1999

It is a pleasure to be here, and to join in marking the chamber's Business Appreciation Month. New Hampshire is a state of small businesses. Many of them here in the North Country are prospering, and this organization has played an important part. I am honored by your invitation.

I am an optimist. I believe that the next century will be a time of incredible prosperity – if we can create an environment where entrepreneurs like you can dream and flourish. A prosperity sustained by low taxes, unleashed by lighter regulation, energized by new technologies, expanded by free trade. A prosperity beyond all our expectations, but within our grasp.

But this hope, in the long-run, depends directly on the education of our children – on young men and women with the skills and character to succeed. So, for the past few months, I have focused on the problems and promise of our public schools.

In September, I talked about disadvantaged children left behind by failed schools. The diminished hopes of our current system are sad and serious – the soft bigotry of low expectations. Schools that do not teach and will not change must have some final point of accountability. A moment of truth, when their federal

51

funds, intended to help the poorest children, are divided up and given to parents – for tutoring or a charter school or some other hopeful option.

Last month, I talked about raising the academic ambitions of every public school in America – creating a culture of achievement. My plan lifts the burden of bureaucracy, and gives states unprecedented freedom in spending federal education dollars. In return for this flexibility, each state must adopt a system of real accountability and high standards. Students must be tested on the basics of reading and math each year – and those results posted, by school, on the Internet. This will give parents the information to know if education is actually taking place – and the leverage to demand reform.

My education proposals are bound by a thread of principle. The federal government must be humble enough to stay out of the day-to-day operation of local schools. It must be wise enough to give states and school districts more authority and freedom. And it must be strong enough to require proven performance in return. The federal role in education is to foster excellence and challenge failure with charters and choice. The federal role in education is not to serve the system. It is to serve the children.

Yet this is only part of an agenda. Yes, we want our children to be smart and successful. But even more, we want them to be good and kind and decent. Yes, our children must learn how to make a living. But even more, they must learn how to live, and what to love. "Intelligence is not enough," said Martin Luther King, Jr. "Intelligence plus character – that is the true goal of education."

So today, here in New Hampshire, I want to make the case for moral education. Teaching is more than training, and learning is more than literacy. Our children must be educated in reading and writing – but also in right and wrong.

Of course, every generation worries about the next. "Children today are tyrants," said one educator. "They contradict their parents, gobble their food, and tyrannize their teachers." And that teacher's name was...Socrates.

Some things don't change. The real problem comes, not when children challenge the rules, but when adults won't defend the rules. And for about three decades, many American schools surrendered this role. Values were "clarified," not taught. Students were given moral puzzles, not moral guidance. But morality is not a cafeteria of personal choices – with every choice equally right and equally arbitrary, like picking a flavor of ice cream. We do not shape our own morality. It is morality that shapes our lives.

Take an example. A Massachusetts teacher – a devoted supporter of values clarification – had a sixth grade class which announced that it valued cheating, and wanted the freedom to express that value during tests. Her response? "I personally value honesty," she said. "Although you may choose to be dishonest, I will insist that we be honest on our tests here. In other areas of your life, you may have to be dishonest."

This is not moral neutrality. It is moral surrender. Our schools should not cultivate confusion. They must cultivate conscience.

In spite of conflicting signals – and in spite of a popular culture that sometimes drowns their innocence – most of our kids are good kids. Large numbers do volunteer work. Nearly all believe in God, and most practice their faith. Teen pregnancy and violence are actually going down. Across America, under a program called True Love Waits, nearly a million teens have pledged themselves to abstain from sex until marriage. Our teenagers feel the pressures of complex times, but also the upward pull of a better nature. They deserve our love and they deserve our encouragement.

And sometimes they show character and courage beyond measure. When a gun is aimed at a seventeen-year-old in Colorado – and she is shot for refusing to betray her Lord. When a seventeen-year-old student, during a madman's attack on a Fort Worth church, is shot while shielding a friend with Downs Syndrome – and continues to comfort her, even after her own injury. We are finding, in the midst of tragedy, that our children can be heroes too.

Yet something is lost when the moral message of schools is mixed and muddled. Many children catch a virus of apathy and cynicism. They lose the ability to make confident judgments – viewing all matters of right and wrong as a matter of opinion. Something becomes frozen within them – a capacity for indignation and empathy. You can see it in shrugged shoulders. You can hear it in the watchword of a generation: "Whatever."

Academics like Professor Robert Simon report seeing many students – nice, well-intentioned young men and women – who refuse to make judgments even about the Holocaust. "Of course I dislike the Nazis," he quotes a student, "but who is to say they are morally wrong?"

At the extreme, in the case of a very few children – lawless, loveless and lonely – this confusion can harden into self-destruction or evil, suicide or violence. They find no elevating ideals – from parents or church or school – to counter the chaos in their souls. "We laugh at honor," said C.S. Lewis, "and are shocked to find traitors in our midst."

But something is changing in this country. Perhaps we have been sobered by tragedy. Perhaps the Baby Boom generation has won some wisdom from its failures and pain. But we are no longer laughing at honor. "Values clarification" seems like a passing superstition. Many states have instituted real character education in their schools, and many more are headed in that direction. After decades of drift, we are beginning a journey of renewal.

Above all, we are relearning a sense of idealism for our children. Parents and teachers are rediscovering a great calling and a heavy burden: to write on the slate of souls.

We must tell our children – with conviction and confidence – that the authors of the Holocaust were evil men, and the authors of the Constitution were good ones. That the right to life, liberty and the pursuit of happiness is not a personal opinion, but an eternal truth.

And we must tell our children – with clarity and certainty – that character gives direction to their gifts and dignity to their lives. That life is too grand and important to be wasted on whims and wants, on getting and keeping. That selfishness is a dark dungeon. That bigotry disfigures the heart. That they were made for better things and higher goals.

The shape of our society, the fate of our country, depends on young men and women who know these things. And we must teach them.

I know this begins with parents. And I know that is easy for a politician to say. Mark Twain once commented, "To do good is noble. To instruct others in doing good is just as noble, and much easier." But the message of our society must be clear. When a man or woman has a child, being a father or mother becomes their most important job in life. Not all teachers are parents, but all parents are teachers. Family is the first school of manners and morals. And the compass of conscience is usually the gift of a caring parent.

Yet parents should expect schools to be allies in the moral education of children. The lessons of the home must be reinforced by the standards of the school – standards of safety, discipline and decency.

Effective character education should not just be an hour a week on a school's virtue of the month. Effective character education is fostered in schools that have confidence in their own rules and values. Schools that set limits, enforce boundaries, teach high ideals, create habits of good conduct. Children take the values of the adult world seriously when adults take those values seriously.

And this goal sets an agenda for our nation.

First, we must do everything in our power to ensure the safety of our children. When children and teenagers go to school afraid of being bullied, or beaten, or worse, it is the ultimate betrayal of adult responsibility. It communicates the victory of moral chaos.

In an American school year there are more than 4,000 rapes or cases of sexual battery; 7,000 robberies; and 11,000 physical attacks involving a weapon. And these are overall numbers. For children attending inner-city schools, the likelihood of being a victim of violence is roughly five times greater than elsewhere. It is a sign of the times that the same security company used by the U.S. Mint and the FBI has now branched out into high-school security.

Surveying this scene, it is easy to forget that there is actually a federal program designed to confront school violence. It's called the Safe and Drug-Free Schools and Communities Act. The program spends about $600 million a year, assisting 97 percent of the nation's school districts.

What's missing from the program is accountability. Nobody really knows how the money is spent, much less whether it is doing any good. One newspaper found that federal money had gone to pay for everything from motivational speakers to clowns to school puppet shows to junkets for school administrators.

As president, I will propose major changes in this program. Every school getting this funding will report their results – measured in student safety. Those results will be public. At schools that are persistently dangerous, students will be given a transfer to some other school – a safe school.

No parent in America – no matter their income – should be forced to send their child to a school where violence reigns. No child in America – regardless of background – should be forced to risk their lives in order to learn.

In the same way, it is a federal crime for a student to bring a gun into any public school. Yet this law has been almost completely ignored by federal prosecutors in recent years. Of some 3,900 violations reported between 1997 and 1998, only 13 were prosecuted. It is easy to propose laws. Sometimes it is easy to pass laws. But the measure of our seriousness is enforcing the law. And the safety of our children merits more than lip service.

Here is what I'll do. We will form a new partnership of the federal government and states – called Project Sentry. With some additional funding for prosecutors and the ATF, we can enforce the law and prosecute the violators: students who use guns illegally or bring guns to school, and adults who provide them. And for any juvenile found guilty of a serious gun offense, there will be a lifetime ban on carrying or purchasing a gun – any gun, for any reason, at any age, ever.

Tougher enforcement of gun laws will help to make our schools safer. But safety is not the only goal here. The excellence of a school is not just measured by declines in robbery, murder, and aggravated assault. Safety is the first and urgent step toward a second order of business – instilling in all of our public schools the virtues of discipline.

More than half of secondary-school teachers across the country say they have been threatened, or shouted at, or verbally abused by students. A teacher in Los Angeles describes her job as "nine-tenths policeman, one-tenth educational." And many schools, intimidated by the threat of lawsuits, have watered down their standards of behavior. In Oklahoma, a student who stabbed a principal with a nail was suspended for three days. In North Carolina, a student who broke her teacher's arm was suspended for only two days.

In too many cases, adults are in authority, but they are not in control.

To their credit, many schools are trying to reassert that control – only to find themselves in court. Generations of movies from The Blackboard Jungle to Stand and Deliver cast as their hero the teacher who dares to bring discipline to the classroom. But a modern version of this drama would have to include a new figure in the story – the lawyer.

Thirty-one percent of all high schools have faced lawsuits or out-of-court settlements in the past two years. This is seriously deterring discipline, and demands a serious response.

In school districts receiving federal school safety funds, we will expect a policy of zero-tolerance for persistently disruptive behavior. This means simply that teachers will have the authority to remove from their classroom any student who persists in being violent or unruly. Only with the teacher's consent will these students be allowed to return. The days of timid pleading and bargaining and legal haggling with disruptive students must be over. Learning must no longer be held hostage to the brazen behavior of a few.

Along with this measure, I will propose a Teacher Protection Act to free teachers, principals and school board members from meritless federal lawsuits when they enforce reasonable rules. School officials, acting in their official duties, must be shielded from liability. A lifetime dedicated to teaching must not be disrupted by a junk lawsuit. We do not need tort lawyers scouring the halls of our schools – turning every classroom dispute into a treasure hunt for damage awards.

Safety and discipline are essential. But when we dream for our children, we dream with higher goals. We want them to love learning. And we want them to be rich in character and blessed in ideals.

So our third goal is to encourage clear instruction in right and wrong. We want our schools to care about the character of our children.

I am not talking about schools promoting a particular set of religious beliefs. Strong values are shared by good people of different faiths, of varied backgrounds.

I am talking about communicating the values we share, in all our diversity. Respect. Responsibility. Self-restraint. Family commitment. Civic duty. Fairness. Compassion. The moral landmarks that guide a successful life.

There are a number of good programs around the country

that show how values can be taught in a diverse nation. At St. Leonard's Elementary School in Maryland, children take a pledge each morning to be "respectful, responsible, and ready to learn." Character education is a theme throughout the curriculum – in writing, social studies and reading. And discipline referrals were down by 70 percent in one year. At Marion Intermediate School in South Carolina, virtues are taught by studying great historical figures and characters in literature. Consideration is encouraged, good manners are expected. And discipline referrals are down by half in one year.

The federal government now spends $8 million on promoting character education efforts. My administration will triple that funding – money for states to train teachers and incorporate character lessons into daily coursework.

We will require federal youth and juvenile justice programs to incorporate an element of character building.

Our government must get its priorities straight when it comes to the character of our children. Right now, the Department of Health and Human Services spends far more on teen contraception than it does on teen abstinence. It takes the jaded view that children are nothing more than the sum of their drives, with no higher goal than hanging out and hooking up. We owe them better than this – and they are better than this. They ask for bread, and we give them a stone.

Abstinence programs show real promise – exactly because more and more teenagers understand that true love waits. My administration will elevate abstinence education from an afterthought to an urgent goal. We should spend at least as much each year on promoting the conscience of our children as we do on providing them with contraception.

As well, we will encourage and expand the role of charities in after-school programs. Everyone agrees there is a problem in these empty, unsupervised hours after school. But those hours should not only be filled with sports and play, they should include lessons in responsibility and character. The federal government already funds after-school programs. But charities and faith-based organizations are prevented from participating. In my administration they will be invited to participate. Big Brothers/Big Sisters, the YMCA and local churches and synagogues and mosques should be a central part of voluntary, after-school programs.

Schools must never impose religion – but they must not oppose religion either. And the federal government should not be an enemy of voluntary expressions of faith by students.

Religious groups have a right to meet before and after school. Students have a right to say grace before meals, read their Bibles, wear Stars of David and crosses, and discuss religion with other willing students. Students have a right to express religious ideas in art and homework.

Public schools that forbid these forms of religious expression are confused. But more than that, they are rejecting some of the best and finest influences on young lives. It is noble when a young mind finds meaning and wisdom in the Talmud or Koran. It is good and hopeful when young men and women ask themselves what would Jesus do.

The measure of our nation's greatness has never been affluence or influence – rising stocks or advancing armies. It has always been found in citizens of character and compassion. And so many of our problems as a nation – from drugs, to deadly diseases, to crime – are not the result of chance, but of choice. They will only be solved by a transformation of the heart and will. This is why a hopeful and decent future is found in hopeful and decent children.

That hope, of course, is not created by an Executive Order or an Act of Congress. I strongly believe our schools should reinforce good character. I know that our laws will always reflect a moral vision. But there are limits to law, set at the boundaries of the heart. It has been said: "Men can make good laws, but laws can not make men good."

Yet a president has a broader influence and a deeper legacy than the programs he proposes. He is more than a bookkeeper or an engineer of policy. A president is the most visible symbol of a political system that Lincoln called "the last best hope of earth." The presidency, said Franklin Roosevelt, is "preeminently a place of moral leadership."

That is an awesome charge. It is the most sobering part of a decision to run for president. And it is a charge I plan to keep.

After power vanishes and pride passes, this is what remains: The promises we kept. The oath we fulfilled. The example we set. The honor we earned.

This is true of a president or a parent. Of a governor or a teacher. We are united in a common task: to give our children a spirit of moral courage. This is not a search for scapegoats – it is a call to conscience. It is not a hopeless task – it is the power and privilege of every generation. Every individual can change a corner of our culture. And every child is a new beginning.

In all the confusion and controversy of our time, there is still one answer for our children. An answer as current as the headlines. An answer as old as the scriptures. "Whatever is true, whatever is honorable, whatever is right, whatever is pure, whatever is lovely, whatever is of good repute, if there is any excellence and anything worthy of praise, let your mind dwell on these things."

If we love our children, this is the path of duty – and the way of hope.

Position Paper
Education: The True Goal of Education

*"Yes, we want our children to be smart and success-
ful. But even more, we want them to be good and kind
and decent. Yes, our children must learn how to make a
living. But even more, they must learn how to live, and
what to love. 'Intelligence is not enough,' said Martin
Luther King, Jr. 'Intelligence plus character – that is the
true goal of education."*

Governor George W. Bush

EXECUTIVE SUMMARY

Governor Bush has developed a comprehensive 3-part education policy, based upon his success in Texas. First, he announced initiatives to close the achievement gap between disadvantaged children and their peers by making schools accountable for results. Schools receiving federal funds that do not teach and will not change will have their federal funds transferred directly to parents to use for tutoring, charter schools, or another option.

Second, Governor Bush has called for creating a "culture of achievement" for all students. His plan will grant states unprecedented freedom from federal regulation in exchange for establishing an accountability system that includes high standards and annual testing to measure performance. Competition would be fostered by empowering parents with information on school performance, and by providing alternatives, such as charter schools and expanded Education Savings Accounts.

The third and final part of Governor Bush's education policy involves initiatives aimed at promoting school safety, classroom discipline, and character development:

To Improve School Safety, Governor Bush will:

• Hold states and districts receiving federal School Safety funds accountable for measuring and demonstrating improved safety.

• Require states and districts to provide all students in persistently dangerous schools with the option of transferring to a safe school.

• Create a uniform system for reporting on school safety and publish the results widely.

• Establish "Project Sentry," a federal-state partnership to prosecute juveniles who bring guns to school or use them illegally, and adults who provide them.

• Ban for life serious juvenile offenders from ever purchasing or carrying a gun.

To Increase Classroom Discipline, Governor Bush will:

• Expect states and districts to establish a "zero tolerance" policy on disruption, empowering teachers to remove violent or persistently disruptive students.

• Enact the "Teacher Protection Act" to shield teachers, principals, and school board members from meritless lawsuits arising from their efforts to maintain discipline.

• Lift legal barriers to information sharing between schools and law enforcement agencies.

To Promote Character Development, Governor Bush will:

• Increase character education funding and incorporate character-building lessons into federal youth programs.

• Establish the "American Youth Character Awards" to honor acts of character.

• Increase federal funding for abstinence programs to a level at least as high as that provided for teen contraception programs.

• Expand the role of faith-based organizations and charities in after-school programs.

School Safety, Discipline and Character

Governor Bush's education policy is based upon a few proven principles of effective school reform:

- Apply pressure from above to set high standards of academic perform- ance.

- Give schools the freedom and flexibility to meet those standards.

- Measure student performance through annual testing, and publish school-by-school results.

- Reward schools whose performance is improving, and impose conse- quences on schools whose performance is stagnating.

- Foster competition from below by empowering parents with information and options.

- Do not give up on any child.

By following these principles, school reformers throughout the United States are proving that schools can change and that standards of excellence can be achieved.

Governor Bush believes that the campaign for excellence in education must be accompanied by a renewed emphasis on character development. He recognizes that moral education must begin at home. But parents have the right to expect schools to be allies in the education of virtue. The lessons of the home must be reinforced by the standards of the school. To meet this chal- lenge, Governor Bush is proposing initiatives to:

- Improve the safety of every child in every public school in America.

- Instill in all our public schools the virtues of discipline, empowering teachers to enforce discipline in their classrooms.

- Promote and honor character development.

Improving the Safety of America's Public Schools

A. Ensure School Safety

The Safe and Drug Free Schools Program (SDFS) is the largest source of federal funding to schools for state and local drug and violence prevention programs. It has provided more than $6 billion to 97 percent of the nation's school districts since its inception in 1986. The program currently provides states and local school districts with $600 million annually.

Unfortunately, SDFS lacks a mechanism to ensure accountability. Indeed, a 1998 *Los Angeles Times* investigation reported that SDFS money has been used by school districts to buy fishing poles, hire magicians, and fund puppet plays.

A 1997 GAO report found that "no overall evaluations of the Safe and Drug-Free Schools Program have been completed." The GAO also concluded that the lack of a uniform method for reporting on school safety made it difficult to maintain federal oversight of the program. Not surprisingly, General Barry McCaffrey, Director of the Office of National Drug Control Policy, has criticized the program for doing little except "mail out checks."

Meanwhile, too many schools in America remain unsafe, too many teachers are threatened by violence, and too many children fear for their safety:

- An estimated three million crimes are committed every year in or near the nation's 85,000 public schools.

- One-fifth of public high schools and middle schools reported at least one violent crime in 1996-1997, the most recent year for which data are available.

- Between 1993 and 1997, teachers were victims of 1,771,000 nonfatal crimes at school, including 1,114,000 thefts and 657,000 violent crimes.

- A 1995 study found that one in three male students attending inner-city schools had been shot at, stabbed, or injured with a weapon at or in transit to school.

To ensure that federal school safety funds achieve results, Governor Bush will:

Hold States and Districts Accountable for Improving School Safety: States and districts receiving School Safety funds will be required to establish standards of school safety and report on safety levels on a school-by-school basis.

Require States and Districts to Provide All Students in Persistently Dangerous Schools with a Transfer to a Safe Alternative: Local education agencies will be required within three years to offer all students in persistently dangerous schools a transfer to a safe public or charter school in the same, or a nearby, district. If no space can be found, the district must use its federal education funding to support a transfer to a private school.

Call for the Creation of a Uniform Reporting System: To allow parents to assess comparative school safety, the federal government will devise a systematic method for reporting and evaluating violence in schools. Data from schools will be widely and regularly disseminated to parents, including by posting information on the Internet.

B. Enforce Juvenile Gun Laws

The federal Youth Handgun Safety Act prohibits anyone under the age of 18 from buying or carrying a handgun. This law also makes it a federal offense to sell or transfer a handgun or ammunition to a minor. In addition, the Gun Free Schools Act requires school districts to expel students who bring a firearm to school.

Unfortunately, these laws have not been aggressively enforced. Indeed, there have been astonishingly few federal prosecutions of juveniles who possess guns, or of the adults who provide guns to juveniles. In fact, from 1997 to 1998:

- Only 11 juveniles were federally prosecuted for possessing a handgun or handgun ammunition.

- Only 13 students were prosecuted under federal law for possessing a firearm in a school zone, though 3,930 were expelled for doing so.

- And only 13 adults were prosecuted under federal law for transferring a handgun or ammunition to a juvenile.

Moreover, no federal law exists to prevent serious juvenile offenders from purchasing or carrying a gun once they become adults. In contrast, adults convicted of a felony are prevented by law from ever again purchasing or carrying a gun in their lifetime.

Governor Bush has already called for more vigorous prosecution of gun offenses. In addition, to deter juveniles from illegally possessing guns and bringing them into schools, and to prosecute adults who provide guns to juveniles, Governor Bush will:

Establish "Project Sentry" to Enforce Federal Juvenile Gun Laws: This federal-state partnership will provide additional funding for state and federal law enforcement to establish local "Safe School Task Forces." These task forces will identify and appropriately prosecute, punish, and supervise juveniles who violate state and federal firearms laws. Each U.S. Attorney's Office would be required to dedicate one federal prosecutor as a "Project Sentry" Coordinator, to ensure juvenile offenders who pose a threat to fellow students are appropriately punished and deterred. The program will also make it a priority to increase prosecutions of gun dealers and adults who illegally purchase guns for juveniles, or who contribute to a person under 18 committing a crime of violence involving a gun.

Impose a Lifetime Ban on Gun Possession for Juvenile Offenders: Any person under the age of 18, who is found guilty of a serious gun or violent offense, will be banned for life from purchasing or carrying a gun.

Enforcing Discipline and Restoring Authority to Teachers

If schools are to set high standards of achievement for students, they must be able to maintain discipline within their classrooms. Persistently disruptive students detract from time that should be spent instructing others. Yet, too many schools in America do not enforce codes of discipline, and teachers and principals are finding it increasingly difficult to maintain order because of legal constraints.

School districts are required by federal law to establish a zero tolerance policy for students that bring guns to school. Almost 80 percent of schools have chosen to establish zero tolerance policies for violence and tobacco use. However, not all schools have a zero tolerance policy for disruptive behavior, allowing teachers to remove from the classroom students who persistently disrupt class. As a result:

- Five out of six principals polled in 1997 said they spent too much time dealing with disruptive students.

- 65 percent of public school teachers charge that discipline is a "serious" problem in their schools.

- 88 percent of teachers think that academic achievement would improve "substantially," if persistent troublemakers were removed from classes.

The problem of enforcing discipline has been compounded by the increasing incidence of lawsuits:

- In the last two years alone, almost one-third of all high school principals reported being involved in lawsuits or out-of-court settlements, versus only 9 percent ten years ago.

- Twenty percent of high school and middle school principals report spending 5-10 hours per week in activities to avoid litigation; six percent report spending as much as 10-20 hours a week doing the same.

- 99 percent of principals say their policy on reporting bad behavior has been modified because of liability costs and concerns.

Finally, federal laws that inhibit the appropriate exchange of information between school officials and local law enforcement officers make it difficult to take effective action against troublesome or violent students. In particular, schools are often unable to provide local law enforcement authorities with information that may help them prosecute a case because federal law severely restricts the circumstances under which such information can be shared.

As President, in order to empower teachers and principals to maintain discipline in the classroom, Governor Bush will:

Remove Barriers to Information Sharing Between Schools and Law Enforcement Authorities: As President, Governor Bush will propose changing federal law to make it easier for public school districts and local law enforcement authorities to share information regarding disciplinary actions and misconduct by students.

Require "Zero Tolerance" Policies for Violence and Persistent Misbehavior: States and districts that receive School Safety funds will be required to impose zero tolerance policies in all schools. While states and districts would be free to design their own policies, at a minimum they will be required to give teachers the authority to remove from the classroom students who engage in violence or persistent misbehavior. These students will be permitted to return to class only with the teacher's consent.

Enact the "Teacher Protection Act": The Teacher Protection Act will shield teachers, principals, and school board members acting in their official capacity from federal liability arising out of efforts to maintain discipline in the classroom, so long as they do not engage in reckless or criminal misconduct. Plaintiffs who bring meritless claims in federal court challenging teacher and principal disciplinary actions would be liable for including attorneys' fees, incurred in the defense of the teachers and principals.

Encouraging Character Development and Moral Education

A. Character Education

Character education promotes the moral development of students by teaching universal virtues. Research indicates that character education can help improve behavior and academic achievement:

- A University of Illinois study of four schools using the "Positive Action" character development program found that the average number of incidents requiring disciplinary referral dropped by 74 percent after one year, and achievement scores improved by an average of 28 percentage points.

- Standardized test scores of students exposed to the "Responsive Classroom" program, which emphasizes good character, increased 22 percent on average, versus just three percent for students not participating in the program.

Though character education has traditionally been a component of American education, the number of schools teaching it has increased over the past few years. More than 70 percent of states support character education through federally funded pilot programs or legislative measures. However, federal funding for character development programs totaled about $8 million in grants for states or districts in FY 1999. In addition, federal regulations limit to 10 the number of states that can receive grants each year.

To encourage the adoption of character education in schools and in federal programs for students, Governor Bush will:

<u>Increase Character Education Funding:</u> As President, Governor Bush will increase funding for character education grants from $8 million to at least $25 million. These grants will be available to states and districts to train teachers how to incorporate character-building lessons and activities in student coursework. In awarding these grants, preference will be given to programs that contain accountability measures (i.e., that monitor a reduction in specific indicators such as cheating or thefts). In addition, he proposes removing the cap on the number of states that can receive character education funding.

<u>Incorporate Character-Building Lessons into Federal Youth Programs:</u> Appropriate federal programs affecting young people, including juvenile justice programs, will be required to teach character education to ensure children in

these programs are learning the importance of modeling good character.

Establish the "American Youth Character Awards" and Rally Support for Character Education: Students who distinguish themselves by acts of character will receive recognition through a presidential certificate. These awards will serve as a focal point for rallying faith-based organizations, youth-serving agencies and America's parents in an effort to restore traditional values in America's young people.

B. Abstinence Education

Numerous nationally recognized studies indicate that abstinence education works not only to reduce teen pregnancy and sexually transmitted diseases, but also to develop good character in young adults. Federal grants are available to establish abstinence programs in schools and community organizations throughout the country. However, the federal government spends twice as much on teen contraception programs (approximately $135 million per year through Title X, Medicaid, and the Adolescent Family Life program) as it does on abstinence education (approximately $62 million per year through Title V and Title XX).

To emphasize the importance of character building through abstinence education, Governor Bush will:

Substantially Increase Funding for Abstinence Education: As President, Governor Bush will increase federal funding for abstinence education to a level at least as high as that provided for teen contraception programs.

C. After-School Programs

Studies indicate after-school programs help reduce drug use, teen pregnancy, and criminal behavior by providing supervised activities during the peak hours for juvenile crime. Many after-school programs, particularly those run by faith-based and community organizations, also incorporate character education into their curriculum.

Unfortunately, federal after-school programs tend to discourage the participation of faith-based groups and other community organizations. For example, under the 21st Century Community Learning Centers program, which is one of the largest federal sources of funding for after-school activities, only schools are eligible to compete for funds. The Administration has recently proposed opening just 10 percent of the program's funding to competitive bidding.

To encourage more after-school programs, Governor Bush:

Open the Entire 21st Century Program to Competition: Governor Bush will introduce legislation to open 100 percent of the 21st Century program's funding to competitive bidding. This will allow youth development groups, local charities, churches, synagogues, mosques and other community and faith-based organizations to compete for these federal funds on an equal footing with schools.

Fund New After-School Programs Using Certificates: Governor Bush will empower lower-income parents by providing them with certificates that can be used to pay for after-school activities of their choosing — whether run by a community group, a neighborhood church, or a local school.

What Others Say

"Like the first two speeches, the grand finale was well-delivered and thought-provoking...the schools Bush envisions are safer, more orderly and more civil. They are places where teachers do not shy away from teaching right and wrong. They put a greater emphasis on abstinence than on contraception, and allow room for children to express their religious views, in art, homework or meetings after school...Bush is also right in arguing that civility must be restored in public schools."

Editorial, <u>Concord Monitor</u>, 11/4/99

"George W. Bush gave one of his best speeches last week in New Hampshire, arguing that the schools have to play a larger role in the moral education of students."

John Leo, <u>U.S. News & World Report</u>, 12/15/99

"[Governor Bush] gave an extraordinarily lucid and powerful speech about character education."

Dr. Michael Josephson, CHARACTER COUNTS!

"The speech, Bush's third on education, was remarkable for its bold conservatism, as he called for teaching morality in the classroom, for allowing religious groups to meet before and after school, to say grace before meals, wear religious symbols, and express religious ideas in art and homework."

Candy Crowley, CNN, "Inside Politics," 11/2/99

"I applaud everything [Governor Bush] said... he is a different kind of politician from the incumbent president, clearly, a better moral example."

Mort Kondracke, <u>Roll Call</u>

THE TEXAS EDUCATION RECORD

Governor Bush has made education his number one priority, both in focus and in funding. Working with the Legislature, he enacted key reforms based on three fundamental principles: local control, limited government and accountability for student performance and achievement.

• Local Control

Governor Bush believes in aligning authority and responsibility at the local level. Power at the local level discourages excuses for failure and encourages accountability and enhanced student performance.

• Limited Government

Governor Bush believes the state's role in education should be limited to setting measurable goals and then holding school districts accountable for achieving those goals. Today, Texas has four clear goals: excellence in math, science, English, and social studies.

• Accountability

Governor Bush believes the state's role in public education is to set clear and measurable goals and to hold districts accountable for results. Under Governor Bush's leadership, Texas has strengthened its accountability system into one of the nation's toughest. Texas now sets goals at the state level and rates individual campuses based on their ability to meet or exceed those goals.

Results: Texas Students Thrive During the Bush Administration

Texas Assessment of Academic Skills (TAAS) test scores have improved significantly for four consecutive years.

- The number of students who passed all parts of the TAAS test has increased 47 percent while Governor Bush has been in office.

- Minority students in particular showed impressive gains – some groups improving their scores by as much as 60 percent.

- Reading performance has improved: 87 percent of all students in grades 3 to 8 and grade 10 passed the reading TAAS in 1998, up from 77 percent four years ago.

Texas students have demonstrated outstanding performance on national evaluations since Governor Bush has been in office:

- On the 1996 National Assessment of Educational Progress (NAEP) in Mathematics, African-American fourth graders in Texas ranked first in the nation among African-American fourth graders, with Hispanic students close behind.

- On the 1998 NAEP Writing Exam, Texas eighth graders ranked fourth in the nation, with African-American and Hispanic eighth-graders scoring first and second in the nation, respectively.

- Texas recently earned the distinction of being one of two states that has made the greatest progress in education in recent years according to the National Education Goals Panel.

Accomplishments

From 1995 through 1999, Governor Bush and the Texas Legislature enacted a series of reforms to establish clear goals, return power to local communities and hold local school districts accountable for educating the children of Texas. Highlights:

- Toughened the Texas accountability system. Under Governor Bush's leadership, Texas has developed its accountability system into one of the nation's strongest and most comprehensive to ensure that no child is left behind.

- Insisted on local control. In 1995, Governor Bush signed a new Education Code that decentralized public education and restored local control to schools.

- Reduced federal education oversight. Texas is one of only 12 states in 1996 to apply for and receive Ed Flex status from the federal government. This status gives educators more freedom in deciding how to use federal education funds.

- Ended social promotion. Governor Bush campaigned for and signed legislation ending social promotion in Texas' public schools. The initiative will help teachers identify and help students who have trouble learning in the earliest grades – when learning problems are easier to fix.

- Implemented the Governor's reading initiative. At Governor Bush's urging, the Legislature appropriated $82 million over a four-year period to help fund reading academies in Texas schools.

- Offered choice in public education. The Texas Legislature, with the support of Governor Bush, authorized the creation of open-enrollment charter schools, including schools for "at-risk" youth. There are currently 168 charter schools approved in Texas.

- Increased funding for education. Texas has increased state funding for public schools by $8.3 billion, representing 56 percent of state spending increases during Governor Bush's tenure. State funding per pupil has increased 37 percent and the state's financial commitment is making it possible for districts to build more than $5 billion worth of new classrooms in Texas.

- Increased teacher pay. The minimum salary for teachers increased 33 percent during Governor Bush's term in office.

Promoting School Safety and Character Education

- Created a Zero-Tolerance Policy for Bad Behavior in Texas Classrooms. In 1995, Governor Bush signed the Safe Schools Act which created two new programs for disruptive students:

  - Juvenile Justice Alternative Education Programs (JJAEP) - Serves expelled students who commit serious or violent offenses in counties with a population of 72,000 or more. Under the program, local juvenile justice boards operate the JJAEPs with guidance from local school districts.

  - Disciplinary Alternative Education Programs (DAEP) - Serves students in all school districts who are removed from their regular classroom due to disruptive behavior or for committing felonies off campus. DAEPs may be located on or off campus.

- Supported the Right Choices Initiative. Governor Bush's "Lone Star Leaders" initiative focuses on key areas proven to boost kids' chances of making the right choices: (1) parental/family connectedness; (2) mentoring; (3) citizenship/character education; (4) abstinence; and (5) after-school programs.

- Lone Star Kids of Character Initiative. On October 22, 1999, Governor Bush awarded $900,000 in funding over a two-year period to support a character-building initiative for Texas school children. The initiative will be one of the largest and most comprehensive character development programs in the nation, providing practical tools to parents, educators, coaches, community and youth organization leaders, and others who want to instill strong character in young people.

What Others Say

"...and on national examinations, Texas schoolchildren have begun to show up their peers in other states. The trend has become so consistent that Texas' public school system, long among the nation's most troubled, is viewed today by educators as an emerging model of equity, progress and accountability."

<u>The New York Times</u>, 5/28/99

"...all I can say is that in Texas, with regard to education, George Bush has managed to maintain the sort of system that ensures attention, support and achievement for minority and poor kids. While he has been governor, the gap between minorities and whites has closed rather remarkably."

Susana Navarro, Executive Director of the El Paso Collaborative for Academic Excellence (a nonprofit group in El Paso, TX)

"In a relatively short period of time, the whole culture of education has changed in Texas. Today, kids of color and poor kids there are fully expected to learn."

Richard F. Elmore, Professor, Harvard University's Graduate School of Education

"By shining a light on the various subgroups at the same time it is raising standards, Texas has managed to pursue both excellence and equity."

"Quality Counts," Education Week Annual Report (Education Week reports major improvements on national and state standardized tests.)

"...within the past few years, Texas has become one of the highest-performing states in the nation. While many educational reform efforts quickly buckle to union pressure or public discontent, Texas' system has only become more rigorous over time. If this trend continues, Texas, one of the nation's poorest states, may soon become the best place to get an education."

<u>Policy Review</u>, March, April 1998.

4

The Duty of Hope:
Armies of Compassion

Indianapolis, Indiana

July 22, 1999

Everywhere I've gone in this campaign – from farms in Iowa to Latino communities in California – I've carried one message. Our country must be prosperous. But prosperity must have a purpose. The purpose of prosperity is to make sure the American dream touches every willing heart. The purpose of prosperity is to leave no one out... to leave no one behind.

We are a wealthy nation. But we must also be rich in ideals – rich in justice and compassion and family love and moral courage.

I am an economic conservative. I believe we should cut taxes to stimulate economic growth. Yet I know that economic growth is not the solution to every problem. A rising tide lifts many boats – but not all. Many prosper in a bull market – but not everyone. The invisible hand works many miracles. But it cannot touch the human heart.

The American Dream is so vivid – but too many feel: The dream is not meant for me. Children abandoned by fathers. Children captured by addiction and condemned to schools that do not teach and will not change. Young mothers without self-respect or education or the supporting love of a husband. These needs are found everywhere, in cities and suburbs and small towns. But the places where these problems are concentrated – from North Central Philadelphia to South Central Los Angeles – have become the ruins of communities. Places where despair is the easy path, and hope the narrow gate.

For many people, this other society of addiction and abandonment and stolen childhood is a distant land, another world. But it is America. And these are not strangers, they are citizens, Americans, our brothers and sisters.

In their hopes, we find our duties. In their hardship, we must find our calling – to serve others, relying on the goodness of America and the boundless grace of God.

The reality here is simple. Often when a life is broken, it can only be rebuilt by another caring, concerned human being. Someone whose actions say, "I love you, I believe in you, I'm in your corner." This is compassion with a human face and a human voice. It is not an isolated act – it is a personal relationship. And it works. The mentors in Big Brothers/Big Sisters – spending only a few hours a week with a child – cut first-time drug use by 50 percent and violent behavior by a third. The success of this fine program proves the obvious: in solving the problems of our day, there is no substitute for unconditional love and personal contact.

I was struck by the story of a gang initiation in Michigan. A 15-year-old boy was forced to stand and take two minutes of vicious beating from other members without fighting back. At the end, he was required to stand up and embrace his attackers. When asked why he submitted to this torture, he answered, "I knew this was going to hurt really bad, but I felt that if I could take it for just a couple of minutes, I'd be surrounded by people who loved me."

Imagine a young life that empty, so desperately in need of real love. And multiply it by millions. This crisis of the spirit creates an expanding circle of responsibility. Individuals are responsible to love our neighbors as we want to be loved ourselves.

Parents must understand that being a good mom or dad

becomes their highest goal in life.

Congregations and community groups must fight for children and neighborhoods, creating what Pope John Paul II calls, "a hospitable society, a welcoming culture."

A president has responsibilities as well. A president can speak without apology for the values that defeat violence and help overcome poverty. A president can speak for abstinence and accountability and the power of faith.

In the past, presidents have declared wars on poverty and promised to create a great society. But these grand gestures and honorable aims were frustrated. They have become a warning, not an example. We found that government can spend money, but it can't put hope in our hearts or a sense of purpose in our lives. This is done by churches and synagogues and mosques and charities that warm the cold of life. A quiet river of goodness and kindness that cuts through stone.

Real change in our culture comes from the bottom up, not the top down. It gathers the momentum of a million committed hearts.

So today I want to propose a different role for government. A fresh start. A bold new approach.

In every instance where my administration sees a responsibility to help people, we will look first to faith-based organizations, charities and community groups that have shown their ability to save and change lives. We will make a determined attack on need, by promoting the compassionate acts of others. We will rally the armies of compassion in our communities to fight a very different war against poverty and hopelessness, a daily battle waged house to house and heart by heart.

This will not be the failed compassion of towering, distant bureaucracies. On the contrary, it will be government that serves those who are serving their neighbors. It will be government that directs help to the inspired and the effective. It will be government that both knows its limits, and shows its heart. And it will be government truly by the people and for the people.

We will take this path, first and foremost, because private and religious groups are effective. Because they have clear advantages over government.

Sometimes the idea of compassion is dismissed as soft or sentimental. But those who believe this have not visited these programs. Compassion is not one of the easy virtues.

At InnerChange – a faith-based program run by Prison Fellowship inside a Texas prison – inmates are up at 5 am and fill their days with work and study rather than soap operas. At Teen Challenge – a national drug treatment program – one official says, "We have a rule: If you don't work, you don't eat." This is demanding love – at times, a severe mercy. These institutions, at their best, treat people as moral individuals, with responsibilities and duties, not as wards or clients or dependents or numbers.

Self-control and character and goal-setting give direction and dignity to all our lives. We must renew these values to restore our country.

Many of these organizations share something else in common: A belief in the transforming power of faith. A belief that no one is finally a failure or a victim, because everyone is the child of a loving and merciful God – a God who counts our tears and lifts our head. The goal of these faith-based groups is not just to provide services, it is to change lives. And lives are changed. Addicts become examples. Reckless men become loving fathers. Prisoners become spiritual leaders – sometimes more mature and inspiring than many of us can ever hope to be.

In Texas, there is a young man named James Peterson, who'd embezzled his way into a prison term. But when he was offered parole, he turned it down, to finish the InnerChange course, which teaches inmates to rely on faith to transform their lives. As James put it, "There is nothing I want more than to be back in the outside world with my daughter Lucy, [but] I realized that this was an opportunity to ... become a living [witness] ... for my brothers [in prison] and to the world. I want to stay in prison to complete the transformation [God] has begun in me."

One example, but a miracle that is common. Sometimes our greatest need is not for more laws. It is for more conscience. Sometimes our greatest hope is not found in reform. It is found in redemption.

We should promote these private and faith-based efforts because they work. But we should also promote them because their challenges are often greater than their resources. Sometimes the armies of compassion are outnumbered and outflanked and outgunned. Visit Mission Arlington in Texas on a day they offer free dentistry, and people are often lined up at 3 or 4 in the morning. Or consider that only 3 percent of America's 13.6 million at-risk children now have mentors. These groups are widespread, but their scale, in some cases, is not sufficient.

It is not enough for conservatives like me to praise these efforts. It is not enough to call for volunteerism. Without more support and resources – both private and public – we are asking them to make bricks without straw.

So today I am announcing a series of proposals. And they are guided by some basic principles.

Resources should be devolved, not just to states, but to charities and neighborhood healers.

We will never ask an organization to compromise its core values and spiritual mission to get the help it needs.

We will keep a commitment to pluralism – not discriminating for or against Methodists or Mormons or Muslims, or good people of no faith at all.

We will ensure that participation in faith-based programs is truly voluntary – that there are secular alternatives.

And we will recognize there are some things the government *should* be doing – like Medicaid for poor children. Government cannot be replaced by charities – but it can welcome them as partners, not resent them as rivals.

Where do we start? Our nation is so prosperous that we can meet our current priorities and still take on new battles. We will strengthen Social Security and Medicare. We will fortify the military. We will cut taxes in a way that creates high-paying jobs. Yet there is another priority. In my first year in office, we will dedicate about $8 billion – an amount equal to 10 percent of the non-Social Security surplus – to provide new tax incentives for giving, and to support charities and other private institutions that save and change lives. We will prove, in word and deed, that our prosperity has a purpose.

My administration will act in three broad areas:

First, we will encourage an outpouring of giving in America. Americans are generous with their time and money. But we can foster that generosity even further – creating fertile ground for the growth of charities.

Right now approximately 70 percent of all tax filers cannot claim the charitable tax deduction, because they do not itemize. We will give people who don't itemize the same treatment and incentive as people who do, rewarding and encouraging giving by everyone in our society, not just the wealthy.

We will provide for charity tax credits – credits which will allow individuals to give a part of what they owe in state taxes directly to private and religious institutions fighting poverty in their own communities. Individuals will choose who conducts this war on poverty – and their support won't be filtered through layers of government officials.

Second, we will involve the armies of compassion in some specific areas of need, to demonstrate how our new approach will work.

Here is an example. America has tripled its prison population in the last 15 years. That is a necessary and effective role of government – protecting our communities from predators. But it has left a problem – an estimated 1.3 million children who have one or both parents in prison. These are forgotten children – almost six times more likely to go to prison themselves – and they should not be punished for the sins of their fathers. It is not only appropriate, it is urgent, to give grants to ministries and mentoring programs targeting these children and their families for help and support. My administration will start bringing help and hope to these other, innocent victims of crime.

As well, we will encourage and expand the role of charities in after-school programs. Everyone agrees there is a problem in these empty, unsupervised hours after school. But those hours should not only be filled with sports and play, they should include lessons in responsibility and character. So we will invite the Boys and Girls Clubs, the YMCA and local churches and synagogues to be a central part of after-school programs.

We will encourage private and religious charities to be more involved in drug treatment and maternity group homes. We will bring programs like InnerChange to four federal prisons, to test if its early promise is fulfilled. And we will set up a compassion capital fund, to identify good ideas transforming neighborhoods and lives and provide seed money to support them – helping to expand the scale of effective programs.

Third, we will change the laws and regulations that hamper the cooperation of government and private institutions. In 1997, Texas officials tried to close down faith-based drug treatment programs because they didn't fit the regulations. When challenged that these programs were effective, one official responded, "We're not interested in results, we're interested in complying with the law." We solved that problem in Texas. If I am president, federal workers in every department of my administration will know that we value effectiveness above red tape and regulation.

We will allow private and religious groups to compete to provide services in every federal, state and local social program. We will promote alternative licensing procedures, so effective efforts won't be buried by regulation. And we will create an advocate position – reporting directly to the president – to ensure that charities are not secularized or slighted.

I visit churches and charities serving their neighbors nearly everywhere I go in this country. And nothing is more exciting or encouraging. Every day they prove that our worst problems are not hopeless or endless. Every day they perform miracles of renewal. Wherever we can, we must expand their role and reach, without changing them or corrupting them. It is the next, bold step of welfare reform.

To take that step, our nation must get beyond two narrow mindsets. The first is that government provides the only real compassion. A belief that what is done by caring people through church and charity is secondary and marginal. Some Washington politicians call these efforts "crumbs of compassion." These aren't "crumbs" to people whose lives are changed, they are the hope of renewal and salvation. These are not the "crumbs of compassion," they are the bread of life. And they are the strength and soul of America.

There is another destructive mindset: the idea that if government would only get out of our way, all our problems would be solved. An approach with no higher goal, no nobler purpose, than "Leave us alone."

Yet this is not who we are as Americans. We have always found our better selves in sympathy and generosity – both in our lives and in our laws. Americans will never write the epitaph of idealism. It emerges from our nature as a people, with a vision of the common good beyond profit and loss. Our national character shines in our compassion.

We are a nation of rugged individuals. But we are also the country of the second chance – tied together by bonds of friendship and community and solidarity.

We are a nation of high purpose and restless reform – of child labor laws and emancipation and suffrage and civil rights.

We are a nation that defeated fascism, elevated millions of the elderly out of poverty and humbled an evil empire.

I know the reputation of our government has been tainted by scandal and cynicism. But the American government is not the enemy of the American people. At times it is wasteful and grasping. But we must correct it, not disdain it. Government must be carefully limited – but strong and active and respected within those bounds. It must act in the common good – and that good is not common until it is shared by those in need.

In this campaign, I bring a message to my own party. We must apply our conservative and free-market ideas to the job of helping real human beings – because any ideology, no matter how right in theory, is sterile and empty without that goal. There must be a kindness in our justice. There must be a mercy in our judgment. There must be a love behind our zeal.

This is where my campaign is headed. We will carry a message of hope and renewal to every community in this country. We will tell every American, "The dream is for you." Tell forgotten children in failed schools, "The dream is for you." Tell families, from the barrios of LA to the Rio Grande Valley: "El sueno americano es para ti." Tell men and women in our decaying cities, "The dream is for you." Tell confused young people, starved of ideals, "The dream is for you."

As Americans, this is our creed and our calling. We stumble and splinter when we forget that goal. We unite and prosper when we remember it. No great calling is ever easy, and no work of man is ever perfect. But we can, in our imperfect way, rise now and again to the example of St. Francis – where there is hatred, sowing love; where there is darkness, shedding light; where there is despair, bringing hope.

Position Paper
Duty of Hope

"We have always found our better selves in sympathy and generosity. Americans will never write the epitaph of idealism. It emerges from our nature as a people, with a vision of the common good beyond profit and loss. Our national character shines in our compassion."

Governor George W. Bush

EXECUTIVE SUMMARY

As President, Governor George W. Bush will commit himself and the nation to mobilizing the armies of compassion – charities and churches, communities and corporations, ministers and mentors – to save and change lives, as he has done in Texas. These groups are proving that real change comes from the bottom up, not the top down.

That is why Governor Bush envisions a different role for government – a role based on the belief that government should turn first to faith-based organizations, charities, and community groups to help people in need. Resources should be devolved, not just to the states, but to the charities and neighborhood healers who need them most and should be available on a competitive basis to all organizations – including religious ones – that produce results. This is the next bold step of welfare reform.

To eliminate barriers to faith-based action and to encourage an outpouring of giving, Governor Bush will:

- Expand "charitable choice" and remove barriers to the participation of faith-based groups in government programs.

- Establish an "Office of Faith-Based Action" in the Executive Office of the President.

- Expand the federal charitable deduction to people who do not itemize.

- Promote a new charitable state tax credit.

- Provide new incentives for corporate giving.

As President, Governor Bush will lead a determined attack on need, launching initiatives to:

- Break the cycle of violence that grips the 1.3 million children of prisoners.

- Open federal after-school programs to community groups, churches, and charities.

- Create a "Compassion Capital Fund" to invest in charitable "best practices."

- Increase drug treatment funding and make faith-based and other non-medical drug treatment programs eligible for federal funds.

- Establish pilot "Second Chance" homes for unwed teenage mothers, and faith-based pre-release programs for prisoners.

- Make permanent the $5,000 adoption tax credit.

Sharing the Dream

America has never been more prosperous. But that prosperity is not shared by all. There is still too much poverty and despair amidst abundance. More than one out of six American families with children live with an income of $17,000 a year or less. There are roughly 14 million young people at risk of not reaching productive adulthood; 1.3 million children with a mother or father in prison; 520,000 children in foster care, more than one-fifth of whom are waiting to be adopted; and, in 1997, over one million babies were born to unwed mothers, 380,000 of whom were under the age of 20.

As President, Governor Bush will commit the country to rallying the armies of compassion nationwide, as he has done in Texas, to ensure no one is left behind as we enter the 21st Century.

A Different Role for Government

Governor Bush believes real change comes from the bottom up, not the top down. Thus, in seeking to help those in need, his administration will look first to faith-based organizations, charities, and community groups that have a track record of success. This is the next bold step in welfare reform.

Governor Bush believes we should support private and faith-based efforts first and foremost because they work. But we should also promote them because the challenges they face are often greater than the resources they possess. He recognizes local efforts lack scale, good intentions often lack resources, and volunteerism alone is not enough. That is why he is proposing a different role for government based on these principles:

- Government should energize private action, not control it, by identifying what works and helping to bring good ideas to scale.

- Resources should be devolved, not just to the states, but to charities and neighborhood healers who need them most.

- Those resources should be made available through contracts, certificates or grants on a competitive basis to <u>all</u> organizations – including religious ones. This competition will spur innovation and better results.

- Organizations receiving resources should not be forced to compromise their core values and spiritual mission.

- Participation in faith-based programs should be truly voluntary, and secular alternatives should exist for beneficiaries.

- Government programs should be committed to pluralism – not discriminating for or against Christians, Muslims, or Jews – or good people of no faith at all.

As President, Governor Bush will follow these principles in mobilizing charities and churches, communities and corporations, ministers and mentors. In the first year of his presidency, Governor Bush will dedicate about $8 billion – an amount equal to 10 percent of the non-Social Security surplus – to provide new tax incentives for giving, and to support charities and other private institutions.

Encouraging an Outpouring of Giving

Americans are a generous people. In 1998, charitable giving totaled $175 billion, an increase of nine percent over the previous year. However, when measured as a percent of gross domestic product, Americans give the same amount today (2.1 percent) as they did in 1971.

Thus, as President, Governor Bush will propose initiatives that will stimulate additional charitable giving by proposing initiatives to:

Expand the Federal Charitable Deduction: Under current law, only people who itemize deductions are allowed to claim a tax deduction for their charitable donations. About 80 million people – 70 percent of all filers – do not itemize. As President, Governor Bush will propose giving every taxpayer the ability to deduct his or her charitable donations. This change will generate billions of dollars annually in additional charitable contributions.

Promote a Charitable State Tax Credit: Governor Bush supports legislation that would provide a credit (of up to 50 percent of the first $500 for individuals and $1,000 for married couples) against state income or other taxes for contributions to charities addressing poverty and its impact. States would be able to designate the charities they want to target with the credit. States would also be permitted – at their option – to offset the costs of this credit by using money from the Temporary Assistance to Needy Families (TANF) program. This optional tax credit would give states additional flexibility in addressing human needs.

Permit Charitable Contributions from IRAs Without Penalty: Under current law, withdrawals from Individual Retirement Accounts are subject to income tax. This creates a disincentive for retirees to contribute some or all of their IRA funds to charity. Thus, Governor Bush supports legislation that would permit individuals over the age of 59 to contribute IRA funds to charities without having to pay income tax on their gifts.

Governor Bush believes corporations must be full partners in the effort to mobilize and strengthen our charities. As President, he will introduce legislation to:

Extend the New Charitable State Tax Credit to Corporations: Governor Bush will allow corporations to participate in the new Charitable State Tax Credit. Under his proposal, corporations will be eligible for a tax credit of 50 percent of the first $1,000 donated to charities dedicated to fighting poverty. In a nation with over five million corporations, this tax credit should help stimulate new partnerships between corporate and social entrepreneurs.

Raise the Cap on Corporate Charitable Deductions: Under current law, a corporation can deduct charitable donations until their value exceeds 10 percent of the company's taxable income. As President, Governor Bush will propose legislation to raise this cap to 15 percent, encouraging firms to raise their giving to charities that address human needs.

Provide Liability Protection for Corporate In-Kind Donations: The 1996 Good Samaritan Food Donation Act protects donors of foodstuffs to charities from liability, except in cases of gross negligence. The 1997 Volunteer Protection Act provided similar protection to individual volunteers. What is lacking is protection for corporate in-kind donations. Many charities, churches, and community groups need vehicles to transport the elderly, computers to educate children, and facilities to hold classes. To encourage such in-kind gifts, Governor Bush supports legislation limiting the civil liability of businesses that donate equipment, facilities, and vehicles to charitable organizations, except in cases of gross negligence.

Eliminating Barriers to Faith-Based Action

Social scientists have documented the power of religion to protect families and change lives. Studies indicate that religious involvement reduces teen pregnancy, suicide, drug abuse, alcoholism, delinquency, and crime. For example, over a decade's worth of "faith factor" research by Dr. David Larson of the National Institute for Healthcare Research and other scholars reveals that poor inner-city youth who attend church are only about half as likely to drop out of school, use drugs, or commit crimes as otherwise comparable youth without religion in their lives.

Similarly, grassroots inner-city outreach ministries have been credited by numerous leading social scientists with playing a major role in helping at-risk youth to avoid violence, achieve literacy, and find jobs. In short, faith-based charities and community groups are proving every day that religion, in the words of UCLA's James Q. Wilson, "creates an opportunity for personal transformation."

In recognition of the growing success of faith-based charities, the 1996 welfare reform bill, which replaced Aid to Families with Dependent Children with Temporary Assistance to Needy Families (TANF), contained a "charitable choice" provision. This provision allowed states to contract with religious organizations "on the same basis as any other non-governmental provider without impairing the religious character of such organizations." Despite this provision, the Administration continues to support regulations that hinder the ability of faith-based charities to provide needed services:

- On September 24, 1998, the U.S. Department of Agriculture notified the Salvation Army's Adult Rehabilitation Center (ARC) in Nashville, Tennessee, that it could no longer act as a food stamp agent, making low-cost, bulk purchases on behalf of the center's residents, because ARC was not certified as a "treatment center." Although the center protested that it was technically a church and provided no medical treatment, USDA forced it to withdraw from the food stamp program. The resulting increase in food costs has forced the center to curtail other services.

- The federal Community Development Block Grant program prohibits, as a general rule, CDBG assistance from being provided to "primarily religious entities for any activities, including secular activities." This prohibition has had a chilling effect on faith-based organizations' willingness to apply for federal funds. According to the executive director of the International Union of Gospel Missions, if these groups have to "strip" their programs of "moral and spiritual aspects, then they wouldn't be worth doing."

Governor Bush believes America must stop trying to eliminate poverty, crime, and addiction with one hand tied behind its back. Thus, he is committed to removing all remaining barriers to the participation of faith-based groups in government programs. As President, he will:

<u>Expand "Charitable Choice:"</u> Governor Bush is committed to making "Charitable Choice" explicitly applicable to all federal laws that authorize the government to use non-governmental entities to provide services to beneficiaries with federal dollars. Participation in faith-based programs should be truly voluntary. Faith-based organizations should be permitted to engage in inherently religious activities – as long as secular alternatives are also available, and those inherently religious activities are privately funded.

<u>Eliminate Other Barriers to Faith-Based Action</u>: Even if "Charitable Choice" is expanded across the board, barriers to the use of federal funds by faith-based groups will remain. Governor Bush believes a concerted effort to identify and remove all such barriers is needed. That is why he will:

- Establish an "Office of Faith-Based Action" in the Executive Office of the President: This office will identify barriers to faith-based action, serve as a national clearinghouse for information on effective faith-based groups, and assist faith-based organizations that need help with regard to federal action.

- Encourage the Establishment of State Offices of Faith-Based Action: Governor Bush will make federal matching funds available to encourage states to establish their own offices to facilitate faith-based action.

- Promote Alternative Licensing Regimes: As President, Governor Bush will promote alternative licensing regimes at the state and federal levels that recognize religious training as an alternative form of qualification.

Examples of the New Approach in Action

New incentives to encourage giving, combined with the elimination of barriers to charitable and faith-based action, form the essential foundation for attacking specific areas of need. The following are examples of just a few of the initiatives Governor Bush will launch as President – initiatives that illustrate a different and innovative approach to empowering the compassionate good work of private organizations and charities.

A. Children of Prisoners: The U.S. prison population has tripled in the past 15 years. On any given day there are 1.2 million people in prison. This has helped protect our communities from predators. But it has left an enormous problem: an estimated 1.3 million children who have a mother or a father – or both – in prison. Studies show that these children are six times more likely to be incarcerated than the average child.

As research by the University of Pennsylvania's John Dilulio and others has shown, too many of these children live in poverty and suffer from the lack of "loving, capable, responsible adults who can teach [them] right from wrong."

Governor Bush believes that these innocent victims of crime should have a special claim on our conscience and on our resources. Unfortunately, there are no federal funds specifically earmarked today for children of prisoners. Thus, as President, Governor Bush will:

Launch an Initiative Directed at Children of Prisoners: This program will make grants available on a competitive basis to faith-based and community groups committed to improving the life prospects of the low-income children of prisoners, through services ranging from church-run preschools to family-rebuilding programs for probationers and ex-prisoners.

B. After-School Programs: Studies indicate after-school programs help reduce drug use, teen pregnancy, and criminal behavior by providing supervised activities during the peak hours for juvenile crime. Unfortunately, some federal after-school programs tend to discourage the participation of faith-based groups and other community organizations. For example, under the 21st Century Community Learning Centers program, which is one of the largest federal sources of funding for after-school activities, only schools are eligible to compete for funds. The Clinton-Gore Administration has recently proposed opening just 10 percent of the program's funding to competitive bidding.

As President, Governor Bush will take a different approach and:

Open the Entire 21st Century Program to Competition: Governor Bush will introduce legislation to open 100 percent of the 21st Century program's funding to competitive bidding. This will allow youth development groups, local charities, and other community and faith-based organizations to compete for these federal funds on an equal footing with schools.

Fund a New After-School Program Using Certificates: Governor Bush will empower lower-income parents by providing them with certificates that can be used to pay for after-school activities of their choosing – whether run by a community group, a neighborhood church, or a local school.

C. Best Practices: Thirty years of social policy have shown that often the most effective efforts have not been large, nationally-directed programs, but smaller, local initiatives. These initiatives are shaped by need, not by bureaucrats. Unfortunately, innovative practices tend to spread slowly because the social marketplace, unlike the commercial marketplace, has no "invisible hand" to promote good ideas, and few financing institutions to help take those ideas to scale.

Thus, to promote "best practices," Governor Bush will:

Establish a Compassion Capital Fund. Governor Bush will establish the Compassion Capital Fund – a public/private partnership that will fund research into "best practices" among charitable organizations, support technical training in those practices, and provide start-up capital to qualified charitable organizations that wish to expand or emulate model programs. He will challenge the private sector to match federal funding of the program.

D. Drug Treatment: Studies show religion is a powerful tool in helping individuals overcome drug and alcohol addiction. However, government regulations tend to view addiction as a disease and prohibit or discourage the licensing of non-medical, faith-based treatment programs.

Governor Bush addressed this problem in Texas by signing legislation exempting programs that do not provide medical treatment, such as Teen Challenge, a nationally-recognized faith-based drug treatment program, from state licensing requirements. Since then, 38 non-medical, faith-based treatment programs have been established under alternative licensing arrangements.

As President, Governor Bush will:

Promote Results-Oriented Drug Treatment Programs: Governor Bush will make performance-based grants for drug treatment programs available to the states and ensure that non-medical, faith-based and community-based organizations are eligible to receive federal drug treatment funds on the same basis as any other organization.

E. Prison Ministries: The power of religion to transform lives has been demonstrated in programs that address everything from drug addiction to domestic violence. This power is now being used to harness change behind prison walls.

The State of Texas has permitted Prison Fellowship Ministries to take over a unit of the state prison in Sugar Land, Texas, and establish "InnerChange" – the nation's first, 24-hour-a-day, Bible and values-based pre-release program, aimed at helping inmates achieve spiritual and moral transformation. Prisoners voluntarily enroll in the program 12 to 18 months prior to release, and receive services for up to 12 months after release.

It is still too early to measure the effectiveness of the InnerChange program. However, there are some positive preliminary indications, and several states are considering implementing similar faith-based programs.

To obtain more data on the effectiveness of these programs, Governor Bush will:

Provide Funding for Pilot Faith-Based Prison Programs: Funding for faith-based pre-release programs will be provided at four federal prisons. To generate substantial data on the efficacy of these programs, projects should be geographically diverse, and include facilities with different levels of security.

F. "Second Chance" Maternity Group Homes: In 1998, over 380,000 unwed mothers under the age of 20 gave birth in the United States. These mothers and their children face extraordinary odds in achieving success. Studies have shown that only about half of these mothers graduate from high school and 80 percent go on welfare. In addition, their daughters are more likely to have children out of wedlock themselves.

The 1996 welfare reform bill requires minor parents to live in an adult-supervised setting in order to receive welfare (TANF) funds. When a conventional adult-supervised setting is not available because of abuse or abandonment by the parent or guardian, federal law requires states to provide or assist in locating alternative living arrangements. Some states have turned to so-called "Second Chance" homes as the alternative. These homes provide young mothers with an opportunity to develop good parenting skills, finish school, and enter the workforce.

Unfortunately, many teenage mothers are placed in a virtually independent living environment because Second Chance homes are not easily available. Indeed, federal regulations currently do not allow federal funds to be used for the purchase or construction of a facility.

Governor Bush believes that to break the cycle of children having children the federal government should:

Fund "Second Chance" Maternity Homes: As President, Governor Bush will provide funding for pilot maternity group homes through a block grant to the states. The states will be authorized to make the funds available either as certificates to individuals, or as competitive grants to providers, who will be able to use the funds to purchase or operate a facility.

G. Foster Care: There are now 520,000 children in foster care, more than one-fifth of whom are waiting to be adopted. Countless more children outside the foster care system are waiting to be adopted into loving families. Although the 1997 Adoption and Safe Families Act did much to move these children to safe adoptive homes, more needs to be done. For example, the cost of adoption still remains a major issue when couples decide to adopt. These costs also may prevent loving, low-income families from considering adoption at all.

Thus, to make adoption more affordable, Governor Bush will:

Make the Adoption Tax Credit Permanent: To help make adoption a more affordable option for families at any income level, Governor Bush will make permanent the current $5,000 adoption tax credit, which would otherwise expire in 2001.

THE TEXAS RECORD

Governor's Faith-Based Task Force

In May 1996, Governor Bush created the "Governor's Advisory Task Force on Faith-Based Community Service Groups" to identify obstacles to faith-based groups and recommend ways Texas can create an environment in which those groups can thrive. In December 1996, Governor Bush signed an executive order directing Texas welfare-related agencies to permit religious-based organizations to compete for state contracts to provide welfare services without sacrificing their distinct religious character.

1997 Legislative Accomplishments

In 1997 the Legislature approved, and Governor Bush signed, several new laws based on recommendations from the Governor's Faith-Based Task Force. These laws encouraged churches, synagogues, and other faith-based groups to offer substance abuse treatment, welfare-to-work services, healthcare, crime-fighting programs, child care and other social services without jeopardizing their religious identity. The Legislature approved measures that:

- Exempt from state licensing and regulation those (non-medical) faith-based alcohol and drug treatment programs that rely exclusively on faith to change lives.

- Permit child care facilities that meet or exceed state standards to be accredited by private sector entities instead of being licensed and regulated by the state.

- Encourage state correctional agencies to use faith-based rehabilitation programs during and after imprisonment.

- Protect from legal liability those who donate medical devices in good faith to nonprofit health care providers.

1999 Legislative Accomplishments

During the recent legislative session, Governor Bush and state lawmakers continued efforts to help faith-based and charitable organizations deliver services to those in need.

- The Texas Religious Freedom Restoration Act which, in response to hostile court cases, strengthens and protects the religious liberty of Texans and limits the government's ability to interfere with a citizen's free exercise of rights.

- A "Good Samaritan" bill that provides liability protections to health care professionals who donates charitable care to needy Texans.

- A law requiring the Texas Department of Human Services to designate certain employees as liaisons to faith-based organizations to promote community services for the needy.

- An exemption from state property tax for charities who help elderly citizens.

- A law directing Texas' 28 local workforce development boards to reach out to religious social ministries.

- A law permitting faith-based groups to acquire the state's surplus and salvage property.

"Charitable Choice" under Governor Bush

The Personal Responsibility and Work Opportunity Reconciliation Act of 1996 included a landmark provision now commonly referred to as "Charitable Choice." Charitable Choice applies when states partner with faith-based and community organizations to deliver welfare services. Governor Bush issued an executive order urging state agencies to use this provision aggressively. And soon a resource guide and series of workshops will be utilized in Texas to train faith-based organizations how to access grants and submit proposals to deliver social services. Under Governor Bush's leadership, Texas leads the nation in implementing Charitable Choice.

Besides the religious groups all across Texas offering government-funded child care to the children of welfare moms, other examples include:

Prison Ministry Programs in Texas

InnerChange
InnerChange is the boldest experiment in criminal rehabilitation ever

attempted in America. It's the nation's first-ever, 24-hours-a-day, Bible and values-based prerelease program, aimed at helping inmates achieve spiritual and moral transformation. Housed at the Jester II unit in Sugar Land, Texas InnerChange is a 3-phase, volunteer-led program that begins 12-18 months before release and continues on for 6-12 months of post-release aftercare to successfully re-integrate inmates back into society. InnerChange is a collaborative effort between Prison Fellowship Ministries, the Texas Department of Criminal Justice, and Houston-area churches.

Texas Youth Commission Pilot Faith-Based Ministry

This year, the Texas Youth Commission began a pilot faith-based dormitory project at the Gainesville State School facility. It's a 12-month structured program for juvenile inmates and their families and uses a spiritually-based curriculum that complements TYC resocialization programs.

Restorative Justice Ministries Network

In response to the Governor's call for faith-based solutions to rehabilitate offenders, the Restorative Justice Ministries Network formed to provide released inmates, via Texas churches and Christian businesspeople, with the tools they need to succeed and reintegrate back into society.

"Second Chance" Teen Parent Program

Created "Second Chance" group homes for unwed teen welfare mothers – run by faith-based and other private groups – to offer them a place to raise their child in a loving, structured environment, get an education and receive job training. The pilot program received $3.3 million in state funding and will serve teen mothers in four Texas counties: Dallas, Harris, Bexar, and Hildalgo. Buckner Children and Family Services, Baptist Children's Home Ministries, and Promise House, three prominent faith-based organizations, won state contracts to operate part of the program.

What Others Say

"If it were a movie it would deserve an Oscar.
"If it were theater it would deserve a five-star rating in the travel guides.
"But it was none of those…it was…Gov. George W. Bush…making his first major policy address.

"Bush has [a] detailed plan to expand the role of faith-based charities and other community groups committed to help the needy.

"Bush deserves high marks for…help[ing] those who have been left behind… it may take…Bush to restore middle-class America's faith in government's ability to help those who need help the most."

Clarence Page, <u>Chicago Tribune</u>, 7/25/99

"Bush's plan moves in the right direction. Churches, temples, and prayer halls cannot replace government in the mammoth task of helping the needy. But they do a better and more efficient job than government of understanding their communities and meeting the needs of their citizens. As Bush wisely points out, they need not be rivals in that task. There is plenty of work to go around."

Editorial, <u>Chicago Tribune</u>, 8/2/99

"In some ways, the new philanthropy ethic dovetails with a growing movement whose focus is using 'faith-based' organizations to move people from welfare to work. Texas Gov. George W. Bush has been on this movement's cutting edge."

**William McKenzie, Associate Editor,
<u>Dallas Morning News</u>, 7/8/97**

5

A Tax Cut with a Purpose

Greater Des Moines Chamber of Commerce

December 1, 1999

From the first day of this campaign, I have been deeply grateful for the warmth and welcome of this state.

Today, I want to share my tax cut plan with you, and with America. A tax cut designed to sustain our nation's prosperity – and reflect our nation's decency.

For nearly twenty years, with rare exceptions, our economy has been strong. America's long economic boom has defied all prediction and precedent.

Twenty-five years ago, experts talked about "limits to growth." We were advised to lower our expectations and ration our dreams. Ten years ago, we were told our country could not compete with the rising economic powers of the world. That we were slipping into the second rank and the second rate.

In America, however, pessimists are seldom prophets. Instead of finding barriers, we have crossed boundaries. Instead of decline, we have seen economic growth beyond all expectation. Consider one fact: For the last 17 years the American economy has created jobs at a pace equal to one new General Motors every four months.

This is a miracle, but not a mystery. The momentum of today's prosperity began in the 1980s – with sound money, deregulation, the opening of global trade and a 25 percent tax cut. And the economic growth of the 1980s provided the venture capital for the technology revolution of the 1990s – creating new wealth out of silicon and genius.

Along the way we have confirmed some truths and discarded some dogmas. Government can be an ally of enterprise – by creating an environment that rewards work and inspires investment. But government does not create wealth. Wealth is the economic measure of human creativity and enterprise. The success of our economy is not a tribute to politicians, hungry for praise. It is a tribute to the effort and risk-taking of Americans. It is a tribute to the power and possibilities of freedom.

But, for America, progress must be more than productivity, and success more than wealth. Even in the best of economic times, we expect more from our country. We want our free society to be a just society.

Everywhere I've gone in this campaign – from farms in this state to Latino communities in California and New York – I've talked about prosperity with a purpose. We want our prosperity to endure. But the purpose of prosperity is to ensure the American dream touches every willing heart – reaches every man or woman who works for a better life.

This is the strength and example of America. Our political system is unique – but so is our economic system. We prize competition and limited government. But we must have other priorities that give direction to our prosperity: social mobility and family and equal opportunity and the entrepreneurial spirit.

We believe in the profit motive – and in the Golden Rule. We are a land of rugged individualists – who are committed to a common good. We want a prosperity as broad and diverse as America itself.

So my tax cut plan is not just about productivity, it is about people. Economics is more than narrow interests or organized envy. A tax plan must apply market principles to the public interest. And my plan sets out to make life better for average men, women and children.

Here are the key elements:

- I will double the current child credit to $1,000 per child.
- I will replace the current five rate tax structure of 15, 28, 31, 36 and 39.6 percent with four, lower rates: 10, 15, 25 and 33 percent.
- I will expand the charitable deduction, allowing taxpayers who do not itemize their returns to deduct contributions.
- I will increase the annual contribution limit on Educational Savings Accounts from $500 to $5,000, and expand them beyond college, down to Kindergarten.
- I will eliminate the death tax.
- I will restore the 10 percent tax deduction for two-income, married couples, greatly reducing the marriage penalty.
- I will eliminate the Social Security earnings test – an unfair burden on working retirees.

These proposals, behind the dry numbers, represent and promote the enduring values of our nation.

Let's start where the need is greatest: with social mobility for hard working American families. We need a tax system that makes it easier, not harder, to join the ranks of the middle class. Half the revenue cost of my income tax cuts goes to financing two changes which I believe are vital for encouraging upward mobility.

I propose we cut the current 15 percent tax bracket by a third – to a 10 percent rate – for the first $12,000 of taxable income for married couples. It's worth recalling that when the income tax was started in 1913, it was intended only for the very rich. It had a top bracket of just 7 percent, then raised to 15 percent. It never occurred to anyone back then to tax the lowest income groups at high rates. But the current tax code does just that. Today, waitresses, store clerks and janitors are paying higher tax rates than were paid by the Morgans, Vanderbilts and Rockefellers of another era.

I also plan to double the child credit to $1,000. This, combined with lower tax rates, can completely eliminate taxes for a four person family earning $35,000 – a tax cut of over $1,500. Many two-income families making $50,000 a year will see their income taxes cut by half.

Single parents will also see their taxes cut drastically. Today, a single parent with one child earning $25,000 per year pays almost $1,500 in income taxes. I will cut that by over two-thirds – over $1,000.

It is not just the amount of taxes that matters, it's also what the economists call a taxpayer's marginal rate: the taxes we pay on every extra dollar we earn. That rate determines the incentives to work.

Under current tax law, for example, a single waitress supporting two children on an income of $22,000 faces a higher marginal tax rate than a lawyer making $220,000. As she moves up, the federal government starts taxing her income at the same time it is reducing her Earned Income Credit benefit. She can work overtime. She can earn a raise. Yet when all taxes are considered, half of her new earnings are taken away. In other words, the hardest hours of labor are taxed at the highest rates.

Under my plan, she will pay no income tax at all. And she will be joined by 6 million other low- and moderate-income, working families, who will be removed from the tax rolls entirely. That is one of every five families in America with children.

We will take down the tollgate on the road to the middle class.

My second goal is to treat the middle class itself with greater fairness.

I propose that we establish a basic principle: No middle-class family should face a federal income tax rate higher than 25 percent.

Many middle class families are working three jobs: his, hers and the full time job of caring for their children. The tax rate cuts and child credit increases in my plan will help. But given their burdens, these families do not need a marriage tax as well. So I propose we restore the marriage tax relief that Ronald Reagan passed in 1981. For a two earner couple, each making $30,000, this will mean eliminating their marriage tax penalty of over $760.

Our society has taxes on alcohol and tobacco and gambling. We call them "sin taxes." But the tax burden on families is a "virtue tax" – discouraging the most important commitments and obligations of life. Under my tax cut plan, families will be rewarded, not punished, for being families.

Securing this measure of fundamental fairness for the middle class accounts for one third of the revenue cost of my income tax changes.

Third, my plan will encourage entrepreneurship – the path to prosperity taken by so many minorities, women and young people.

Across America, more than 1 in 5 jobs is created by a business that didn't exist a decade ago. And the story of this success is written in many hands. Between 1987 and 1997, the number of Hispanic-owned businesses more than tripled... African-American and Asian-owned businesses more than doubled. Since the 1970s, women's share of small business ownership increased from 5 percent to 38 percent.

One basic problem: Many of these hard working risk-takers find that government expects to be a partner in their success – sharing none of the risks, but nearly half of the profits.

Let us lay down another basic principle: No one in America should have to work more than 4 months a year to pay the IRS. The federal government, in peacetime, has no business taking more than 33 percent of anyone's paycheck. After all, the entrepreneurs of

America create jobs, take risks and make their profits with honor. My tax cut plan will expand their ranks by encouraging American enterprise, not penalizing it.

Setting the top tax rate at 33 percent will take about one dollar of every six of the revenue cost of my income tax reductions. Entrepreneurs and small business owners are also singled out for punishment by the estate tax – better known as the "death tax."

Right now, as every farmer knows, inheriting a family business generally means inheriting a tax, on assets over $650,000, of between 37 and 55 percent. Family businesses often can't afford this. They may have assets, but lack ready cash. Many inherited businesses fail. In nine of ten cases, the heirs list the death tax as a major cause.

The death tax penalizes those who want to build on the wealth created by their family. It impedes economic growth by seizing the capital needed to make small businesses flourish. It can tax wealth three times over – in the earning, in the transfer, and in the sale of an asset.

When a man or woman builds a business, they are also leaving a legacy. Their death should not mean the end of their life's work. This tax violates virtually every principle of common sense and free enterprise – and I intend to abolish it.

Fourth, my plan takes the side of compassion and giving – because a prosperous society must be a generous society.

A rising tide lifts many boats, but not all. Many prosper in a bull market, but not everyone. In the most affluent country of history, there are still people in need of help and hope. And there are private and religious groups in every community willing to provide both – saving children from gangs, rescuing people from addiction, caring for women in crisis.

Yet it is not enough for conservatives like me to praise these efforts. It is not enough to call for volunteerism. Without more support and resources, both private and public, we are asking them to make bricks without straw.

Most of these groups depend on charitable contributions. Yet today 70 percent of tax filers cannot claim the charitable deduction, because they do not itemize. Under my plan, people who don't itemize will be given the same treatment and incentive as people who do, rewarding and encouraging giving by everyone in our society, not just the wealthy.

Finally, we must treat the elderly with dignity.

Our "greatest generation" deserves our greatest respect.

This begins by keeping our word. We must protect Social Security benefits for those who receive them... reserve the Social Security surplus for Social Security itself... while giving young workers of today new options like personal retirement accounts. A reform that would strengthen the system and give workers a larger share in the economic growth of America.

Respecting seniors also means respecting their abilities. Our current system places little value on the economic potential of senior citizens, as if their productive years were just a fading memory. Under today's "earnings test," as it's known, many Social Security recipients who continue to work lose anywhere from 33 to 50 percent of their benefits. An effective tax rate of up to 70 percent.

I happen to know two senior citizens very well. And neither of them shows much inclination to withdraw from productive life. One of them, at the age of 64 was elected President of the United States. At 75, he jumped out of an airplane. Both today keep busy. But my parents are just one example of the millions of skilled and experienced seniors who still have a lot to offer their community and their country.

Congress has made some adjustments in this earnings test. My plan eliminates it entirely – a change that will help millions of seniors. The law should not hinder our seniors from making their own choices and working as long as they want – all while fully receiving the Social Security benefits they have already earned.

These five priorities – social mobility, middle class families, entrepreneurship, charity and the elderly – mark a very different direction from that of the current administration. It has increased the level of taxes. And the percentage of national income we now pay in federal income taxes is the highest since the Second World War, when America had eight million men under arms. Yet the President and Vice President insist that tax cuts are a "risky" proposition.

I do not accept the assumption that it is somehow "risky" to let taxpayers keep more of their own money.

What is risky is when politicians are given charge of a surplus. There is a strong temptation to spend it. And, in Washington, that temptation is overwhelming. A government with unlimited funds soon becomes a government of unlimited reach.

There are only two things that can be done with a surplus. It can be used by government, as the president proposes. Or it can be used by Americans, to save and build and invest. As you can see from this tax plan, I have made my choice. I choose the creation of wealth, over the care and feeding of government.

I am always amazed when I hear politicians say government cannot "afford" a tax cut. May I remind them that government does not "pay" for anything: The people pay for government. The question is not how much government can afford to give to taxpayers. The question is how much the taxpayers can afford to give to government.

Low tax rates are a powerful economic tool to promote a higher standard of living for all Americans. They can be the difference between renting or buying a home, paying or postponing a debt, saving for college or worrying you won't be able to help your children.

Yet I also believe in tax cuts for a another practical reason: because they provide insurance against economic recession.

Sometimes economists are wrong. I can remember recoveries that were supposed to end, but didn't. And recessions that weren't supposed to happen, but did. I hope for continued growth – but it is not guaranteed. A president must work for the best case, and prepare for the worst.

There is a great deal at stake. A recession would doom our balanced budget. It would leave far less money to strengthen Social Security and Medicare. But, if delayed until a downturn begins, tax cuts would come too late to prevent a recession. Putting more wealth in the hands of the earners and creators of wealth – now, before trouble comes – would give our current expansion a timely second wind.

Our times allow a substantial tax cut. Integrity requires that it also be a realistic and responsible tax cut.

My plan is realistic because it avoids meaningless 15-year budget projections. It is not based on inflated growth estimates.

It is easy to build false hopes with false numbers. But this is not daring, it is deception. It is not boldness, it is cynicism. And Americans see through it.

For me, tax cutting is not some abstract cause. I have a plan, but I also have a record. I have actually done the work of passing tax cuts. Of persuading Democrats and Republicans to join in the two largest tax reductions in Texas history – nearly $3 billion returned to taxpayers.

My tax cut plan for America is responsible because it sets priorities. It reserves all the Social Security surplus for Social Security itself. None of it will be used either for new spending or tax reductions. My plan balances the budget. It funds needed priorities, including defense and education. It reduces the national debt. And it ensures that the excess – the rest of the surplus – is returned to the American people, who earned it and deserve it.

These, then, are the basic ideas that guide my tax policy: lower taxes for all, with the greatest help for those most in need. Everyone benefits – while the highest percentage tax cuts go the lowest income Americans.

This plan is judicious in approach – using real numbers. And just in effect – helping real people.

I believe this is a formula for continuing the prosperity we've enjoyed, but also expanding it in ways we have yet to discover. It is an economics of inclusion. It is the agenda of a government that knows its limits and shows its heart.

For many years "sharing wealth" was a code word for redistribution – the project of government planners and social engineers. With the best intentions, they actually added to the sum of suffering.

My economic vision goes in the opposite direction. I believe our sustained prosperity now permits us to use the tools of the free market to promote the goals and values we share as a nation: independence, accountability, faith in the good judgement of citizens, confidence in their ability to compete, and charity for those who cannot.

How fortunate we all are to live in an age and a country where effort is rewarded, freedom prized and opportunity shared. Now let us press on, making the most of this chance given to no other nation in no other time – building a country rich not only in goods, but in goodness, and not only the envy of the world, but its inspiration.

Position Paper
A Tax Cut with a Purpose

"These, then, are the basic ideas that guide my tax policy: lower taxes for all, with the greatest help for those most in need. Everyone benefits – while the highest percentage tax cuts go to the lowest income Americans. This plan is judicious in approach – using real numbers. And just in effect – helping real people. I believe this is a formula for continuing the prosperity we've enjoyed, but also expanding it in ways we have yet to discover. It is an economics of inclusion. It is the agenda of a government that knows its limits and shows its heart."

Governor George W. Bush

EXECUTIVE SUMMARY

Federal taxes are the highest they have ever been during peacetime. High taxes unfairly limit the participation of low-income earners, middle-class families, and seniors in today's prosperity, and act as a success tax on entrepreneurs. That is why Governor Bush has developed a bold tax cut plan.

Governor Bush's tax plan will convert the income tax code into a simpler, flatter, and fairer tax system. His approach focuses on reducing marginal rates to spur and sustain economic growth:

- The current five-rate tax structure of 15, 28, 31, 36, and 39.6 percent will be replaced with four lower rates: 10, 15, 25, and 33 percent.

This new, flatter rate structure will mean lower taxes for all working Americans. Because Governor Bush believes that a free society must also be a just society, the highest percentage cuts will go to those families and individuals with the lowest incomes *(see Chart 1)*.

Recognizing that prosperity should have a purpose, the Bush tax cut plan focuses on five priorities:

- Increasing access to the middle class for hard-working families by creating a new 10 percent bracket and doubling the child tax credit.

- Treating all middle class families with greater fairness by lowering the top middle class rate to 25 percent, raising the threshold for the phase-out of the child tax credit, and greatly reducing the marriage penalty.

- Encouraging entrepreneurship and growth by cutting the top marginal tax rate to 33 percent, eliminating the death tax, and making the R&D tax credit permanent.

- Promoting charitable giving and education by allowing non-itemizers to deduct charitable contributions, and by expanding Education Savings Accounts.

- Allowing seniors to work without penalty by eliminating the Social Security earnings test.

Governor Bush's tax cuts will be financed exclusively out of the non-Social Security surplus:

- Governor Bush supports Social Security "lock box" legislation, which will wall off the Social Security surplus from the rest of the budget.

The baseline economic projection underlying the plan assumes a realistic growth rate of 2.7 percent – considerably lower than the recent experience:

- Under the baseline projection, the Bush income tax cuts will be phased in over five years – the official horizon of the President's budget.

CHART 1

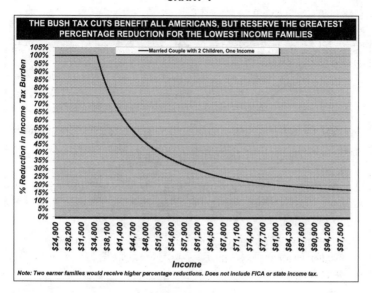

THE BUSH TAX CUTS BENEFIT ALL AMERICANS, BUT RESERVE THE GREATEST PERCENTAGE REDUCTION FOR THE LOWEST INCOME FAMILIES

Married Couple with 2 Children, One Income

% Reduction in Income Tax Burden

Income

Note: Two earner families would receive higher percentage reductions. Does not include FICA or state income tax.

★ ★ ★

Increasing Access to the Middle Class for Working Families

The current tax code's high marginal rates serve as a barrier to the middle class for many low income families. Because the benefit of the Earned Income Credit diminishes as workers earn more, many families face punitive marginal rates that serve as a powerful disincentive to assume extra responsibility at the office, work an extra shift, take technical training, or invest in a higher educational degree.

Thus, to provide a greater reward for those who make the sacrifices needed to move ahead, one-half of the revenue cost of the Bush income tax cuts would finance changes designed to help low-income families enter the middle class. Specifically, Governor Bush's tax cut plan will:

<u>Substantially Lower the Marginal Tax Rate for Low Income Parents</u>: Under the Bush tax cut plan, the marginal income tax rate would fall by over 40 percent for low income families with two children, and by nearly 50 percent for fam-

CHART 2

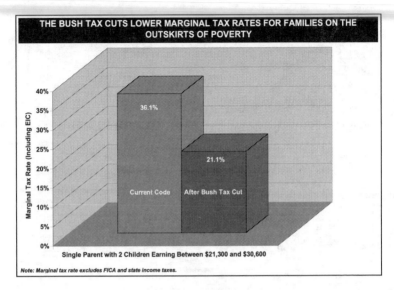

THE BUSH TAX CUTS LOWER MARGINAL TAX RATES FOR FAMILIES ON THE OUTSKIRTS OF POVERTY

Single Parent with 2 Children Earning Between $21,300 and $30,600

Note: Marginal tax rate excludes FICA and state income taxes.

CHART 3

THE BUSH TAX CUTS REMOVE OVER SIX MILLION LOWER AND MODERATE INCOME FAMILIES FROM THE FEDERAL TAX ROLLS

Filing Status	Current Tax Code	After Bush Tax Cuts
Married Filers:*		
Married with 1 Child	$18,800	$26,200
Married with 2 Children	$24,900	$36,500
Single Filers:		
Head of Household w/ 1 Child	$15,200	$21,900
Head of Household w/ 2 Children	$21,300	$31,300
Single Filers	$7,100	$7,100
TOTAL FILERS REMOVED FROM THE TAX ROLLS:		**6 MILLION**

Minimum Income Before Paying Income Taxes

*Assumes two earner family with top earner making 75% of their combined income.
Note: Does not include EIC, FICA, or state income taxes. (Based on 2002 filer data estimates).

ilies with one child *(see Chart 2)*. This results from two key changes in the tax code:

- The current 15 percent tax bracket will be cut to 10 percent for the first $6,000 of taxable income for singles, the first $10,000 for single parents, and the first $12,000 for married couples; and

- The existing child tax credit will be doubled to $1,000.

As a result of these changes, six million families – one in five taxpaying families with children – will no longer pay any federal income tax *(see Chart 3)*.

Treating All Middle Class Families More Fairly

Governor Bush believes it is imperative to ease the excessively high tax burden on middle class and upper middle class families – a burden that robs families of precious time together and resources to address pressing needs. As a result, one-third of the revenue cost of the plan's income tax cuts is related to changes that treat these families more fairly. These changes make the tax code pro-children and pro-marriage.

Specifically, Governor Bush's tax cut plan will:

Cut the Maximum Marginal Rate for the Middle Class to 25 Percent: A new, lower maximum marginal tax rate of 25 percent will be established for the middle class. This 25 percent rate will apply to married couples with taxable income over $43,050 and to singles with taxable income over $25,750. Currently, these taxpayers face a marginal rate of 28 or 31 percent.

Greatly Reduce the Marriage Penalty: The marriage penalty will be cut by restoring the deduction for two-earner families. This will allow the lower-earning spouse to deduct 10 percent – up to $3,000 – of the first $30,000 of income. If each spouse earned $30,000, the marriage penalty will drop from $763 under the current code to $0 under the Bush code. On average, the two-earner deduction will eliminate roughly half of the marriage penalty for couples with combined incomes between $50,000 and $100,000. The marriage penalty will be further mitigated by the effect of the new, lower maximum rate of 25 percent, which will reduce the portion of the marriage penalty that derives from a progressive rate structure.

Raise the Threshold for the Phase-Out of the Child Credit: The starting point for the phase-out of the child tax credit will be raised from $110,000 to

$200,000 for married couples, and from $75,000 to $200,000 for single parents.

As a result of these changes, a family of four earning $50,000 will receive about a 50 percent tax cut (returning over $1,900), and a family of four earning $75,000 will receive about a 25 percent tax cut (returning over $2,500).

Encouraging Entrepreneurship and Growth

Reducing marginal tax rates is the best way to promote economic growth through the tax code. Reducing the top rate in particular would spur entrepreneurial activity and help attract the best workers from around the globe to America.

Governor Bush believes it is critical to reduce taxes on entrepreneurial success in order to help expand the economy through innovation. That is why one-sixth of the cost of the Bush income tax cuts would go toward eliminating the success tax on entrepreneurs and creators of wealth. Specifically, the Bush tax cut plan will:

Cut the Top Marginal Tax Rates: The maximum marginal tax rates of 36 and 39.6 percent will be cut to 33 percent. This reduction should provide a powerful economic stimulus to the economy over time.

High marginal tax rates are not the only limitation on wealth creation and risk-taking. The death tax also impedes economic growth because much of the capital formation in America occurs through estates. More capital means more tools and higher incomes for all workers. Since the marginal federal tax rate on savings can reach 73 percent (the 40 percent top income tax rate combined with the effect of the 55 percent top death tax rate), the death tax can also create a disincentive for seniors who want to save for their children or grandchildren.

The punitively high death tax falls most heavily on small businesses and family farms that are land rich but cash poor. According to a 1993 survey, nine of ten successors whose family businesses failed within three years of the owner's death listed the death tax as a contributing factor.

Further, by encouraging tax avoidance through trusts and life insurance, the death tax may actually lower income tax revenue more than it raises death tax revenue. The tax has created an entire industry of lawyers and accountants. Compliance costs can reach 65 cents for every dollar raised in revenue, making this one of the most inefficient federal taxes.

Governor Bush believes that the bias of the death tax against the family farm and family business is the antithesis of the American Dream. Accordingly, the Bush tax cut plan will:

Eliminate the Death Tax: Eliminating the death tax will allow family farms and businesses to be passed from one generation to the next without having to break up or sell the assets to pay a punitive tax to the federal government. As a result, wealth would be taxed once – when it is earned, not again when entrepreneurs and senior citizens pass the fruits of their labors to the next generation.

A final impediment to innovation and economic growth is the uncertainty surrounding whether the current Research and Development tax credit will continue to exist. The R&D tax credit was originally enacted in 1981 and provides companies with a 20 percent tax credit for incremental R&D expenditures. According to one study, the credit yields a 31 percent return on investment – more than twice the rate of typical incentives. However, extensions of the tax credit have resulted in three gaps in coverage, two of which were retroactively filled. The on-again, off-again nature of the tax credit impedes long-term research.

To encourage research, the Bush tax cut plan will:

Make the R&D Tax Credit Permanent: To create an environment that rewards investment in innovative technologies, the existing Research and Development tax credit will be made permanent. This should spur the sustained, long-term investment in R&D that America needs to develop the next generation of critical technologies – both civilian and military.

Promoting Charitable Giving and Education

Governor Bush believes that a prosperous society must be a generous society. Since the tax code first began in 1913, the law has recognized the importance of encouraging charitable giving by providing a deduction. Today, however, 70 percent of all filers – about 80 million people – cannot deduct their charitable donations because they do not itemize deductions. **Thus, to encourage an outpouring of giving, the Bush tax cut plan will:**

Expand the Federal Charitable Deduction: As President, Governor Bush will propose giving every taxpayer the ability to deduct his or her charitable donations. This change will generate billions of dollars annually in additional charitable contributions.

Permit Charitable Contributions from IRAs Without Penalty: Under current law, withdrawals from Individual Retirement Accounts are subject to income tax. This creates a disincentive for retirees to contribute some or all of their IRA funds to charity. Thus, Governor Bush supports legislation that would permit individuals over the age of 59 to contribute IRA funds to charities without having to pay income tax on their gifts.

Raise the Cap on Corporate Charitable Deductions: Under current law, a corporation can deduct charitable donations until their value exceeds 10 percent of the company's taxable income. As President, Governor Bush will propose legislation to raise this cap to 15 percent, encouraging firms to increase their giving to charities that address human needs.

Governor Bush's tax cut plan will also generate more resources for education. His plan recognizes that whether their children attend public, private, religious, charter or home schools, parents need funds to pay fees, buy books and supplies, cover transportation costs, and pay for tutoring and special needs.

In principle, education savings accounts should empower parents, allowing parent-directed dollars to be applied to specific problems. However, the current education savings accounts – which permit parents to contribute $500 annually and to withdraw those dollars tax free – can only be used to pay for college and other higher education expenses. **Thus, to empower parents with additional education resources, Governor Bush's tax cut plan will:**

Expand Education Savings Accounts: Governor Bush will allow families or individuals with incomes up to $150,000 (or single earners with annual incomes up to $95,000) to contribute up to $5,000 annually per child into education savings accounts. Parents will be permitted to withdraw funds tax free (i.e., without being taxed on any gain or interest earned) to use for education-related purposes – from kindergarten to college.

Allowing Seniors to Work Without Penalty

Under current law, Social Security recipients who continue to work lose a portion of their benefits due to the Social Security earnings test. Those who are age 62 to 64 lose $1 of benefits for every $2 they earn over $9,000, and those who are age 65 to 69 lose $1 of benefits for every $3 they earn over $15,500. This work penalty adds between 33 and 50 percentage points to the already high marginal rates in the income tax code. For this reason, the earnings test discourages Social Security beneficiaries from working.

Governor Bush believes America's seniors should be allowed to contribute to society for as long as they choose without penalty. Thus, the Bush tax cut plan will:

Repeal the Social Security Earnings Test: According to the Social Security actuaries, eliminating the work penalty would have little impact on the long-run financial status of the Social Security trust fund. By encouraging seniors to work longer, the repeal of the earnings test would boost Social Security tax revenue, increase general tax revenue, and decrease Medicare payments. Over time, these factors will more than offset the increase in Social Security benefits.

Distributional Impact of Governor Bush's Tax Cuts

Governor Bush's tax cuts will reduce income taxes for all Americans, but will especially benefit lower and middle-income families. For example, under the current code, a typical married couple with two children begins paying federal income taxes when their earnings reach $24,900. Under the Bush tax cut, this family would not begin paying taxes until its earnings reached $36,500. Similarly, under the current code, a single mother with two children begins paying taxes when she earns as little as $21,300. But under the Bush plan she would not become a taxpayer until her earnings reached $31,300 a year *(see Chart 3)*. Many other lower-income taxpayers will see their income taxes slashed by over 50 percent. More affluent Americans also receive a tax cut, but they will also shoulder a larger portion of the federal income tax burden *(see Chart 4)*. The result is an income tax burden that is fairer, yet lowers income taxes for all taxpayers.

Financing the Tax Cuts

A. Locking Up the Social Security Surplus

Governor Bush is committed to ensuring that all of Social Security's money is preserved for Social Security. That is why he is a strong supporter of Social Security "lock box" legislation, which would wall off the Social Security surplus from the rest of the budget. The "lock box" would ensure that all Social Security money is dedicated to paying benefits to current and future recipients and to modernizing the program for future generations. Thus, as President,

Governor Bush would finance his tax cuts exclusively out of the "on-budget," or non-Social Security surplus.

CHART 4

UNDER THE BUSH TAX CUT PLAN, LOWER AND MIDDLE INCOME FAMILIES WILL SHOULDER LESS OF THE INCOME TAX BURDEN		

Tax Burden by Income Bracket for 2004

	PERCENT OF TOTAL INCOME TAXES PAID		Percent Cut In Income Tax Burden
	Current Tax Code	**After Bush Tax Cuts**	**After Bush Tax Cuts**
Less than $10,000	-0.9%	-1.1%	100.0%
$10,000 to $20,000	-1.0%	-1.4%	100.0%
$20,000 to $30,000	2.2%	1.9%	28.3%
$30,000 to $40,000	4.1%	3.8%	20.1%
$40,000 to $50,000	5.4%	5.1%	17.9%
$50,000 to $75,000	14.6%	14.2%	15.8%
$75,000 to $100,000	13.6%	13.4%	14.6%
$100,000 to $200,000	22.8%	23.2%	12.1%
$200,000 and over	39.1%	40.9%	9.7%
Total, All Taxpayers	100.0%	100.0%	

Note: Distribution assumes that the Bush Plan is fully phased-in. Does not include the charitable deduction or the expansion of the education savings accounts, but does include EIC payments.

B. Conservative Budget Assumptions

Because budget forecasts are subject to substantial uncertainty, Governor Bush believes it is important to err on the side of caution. For example, in recent years the White House Office of Management and Budget and the Congressional Budget Office (CBO) have understated the budget surplus four years into the future by an average of about $200 billion. Thus, Governor Bush's tax cut plan is based on the following conservative assumptions:

- Real economic growth will average 2.7 percent over the long run. This rate is lower than the average growth rate since 1981 and is considerably lower than the four percent real growth rate of the last three years. The 2.7 percent rate is also identical to the long-term Blue Chip consensus estimate, a compilation of 50 of the top private forecasters.

- Spending will exceed the CBO forecast. The Governor's baseline surplus projection reflects the fact that the President and the Congress have exceeded the budget caps set by the Balanced Budget Act of 1997 by about $32 billion. However, not all of this $32 billion represents a permanent addition to the budget baseline. Indeed, at least $15 billion in appropriations are one-time expenses, including payments for the Census, Y2K upgrades, the Wye River agreement, emergency farm aid, and UN arrears payments. The remaining $17 billion of spending is built into Governor Bush's baseline projection because it is for recurring expenses, such as overseas defense operations and natural disasters.

- <u>The projection does not take account of any likely economic feedback.</u> Governor Bush's tax cuts will accelerate economic growth by making the economy more efficient and more productive. The additional revenues from this growth have not been counted as a means of financing the tax cut. This assumption is in accordance with the methodology of the Congressional Joint Committee on Taxation (JCT).

- <u>The projection does not take account of any behavioral feedback from the tax cuts.</u> Also in accordance with JCT methodology, the additional revenue from predictable changes in taxpayer behavior induced by the tax cut plan have not been counted as a means of financing the tax cuts. As rates come down, taxpayers tend to shift more income into taxable forms and also decrease the use of complex tax shelters. In fact, the economic evidence is overwhelming that the Bush tax cut plan will cost significantly less than the static revenue estimates suggest.

C. Financing the Tax Cuts Out of the Non-Social Security Surplus

Governor Bush's tax cut plan would return $483 billion to taxpayers over five years. The conservative budget assumptions used in this plan produce a projected on-budget surplus of $586 billion. Thus, while the *actual* surplus could easily be $250 billion higher, even the *projected* on-budget surplus is sufficient to finance Governor Bush's tax cuts without dipping into the Social Security surplus.

Examples of the Bush Income Tax Cut

A single parent with 2 children making $25,000 will receive a 100% reduction.

A single parent with 2 children making $40,000 will receive a 53% reduction.

A family of four making $35,000 will receive a 100% income tax reduction.

A family of four making $50,000 will receive a 50% income tax reduction.

A family of four making $75,000 will receive a 25% income tax reduction.

What Others Say

"The most important work of the next American President will be nurturing today's painfully earned prosperity. With the tax-cut proposal he unfurls today, George W. Bush sends his strongest signal to date that he understands this challenge. . . Mr. Bush is proposing an economic agenda worthy of a new President."

Editorial, <u>Wall Street Journal</u>, 12/01/99

". . . 'These are Reaganite across-the-board cuts. This is a bold decision to abolish the death tax, to eliminate the earnings test on seniors, which has been a Republican goal for 40 years now, and it's a great giant step forward towards fundamental reform.'"

**National Public Radio, Grover Norquist,
President of Americans for Tax Reform,12/01/99**

". . . the plan operates within the confines of political reality and a conservative belief that lasting prosperity requires opportunities for all Americans to earn and save without excessive government tithes. . .Mr. Bush also would phase out the burdensome estate tax and lessen the tax burden on married couples. . . The program Mr. Bush has laid out is worth fighting for."

Editorial, <u>Dallas Morning News</u>, 12/02/99

"...a different kind of Republican – one willing to offer sizable tax reductions for the working poor, proposing to take 6 million American off the tax rolls by cutting the lowest tax rate to 10 percent from 15 percent."

Neikirk, <u>Chicago Tribune</u>, 12/02/99

"...the most sweeping tax cut since Gov. Ronald Reagan offered the 1980 tax cut that transformed our economy. Mr. Bush's tax cut drives at the weakest part of our tax system, the high, incentive-destroying tax rates paid by those on the outskirts of poverty."

Martin Anderson, Editorial, <u>Washington Times</u>, 12/03/99

What Others Say

"Texas governor's approach was more reminiscent of Ronald Reagan..."

Editorial, <u>The New York Times</u>, 12/4/99

"Mr. Bush's plan is a good one. Because it emphasizes cutting marginal tax rates, it would significantly improve the economy's performance as well as increase after-tax incomes...The projected long-term budget surpluses present a remarkable opportunity to reduce marginal tax rates once again and to do so without creating budget deficits. It is an opportunity that should not be missed."

Martin Feldstein, Editorial, <u>Wall Street Journal</u>, 12/6/99

"The important thing is that it touches all the...bases...substantial enough that it means something to the people who he feels need to be given something in the tax area." (Bruce Bartlett, former Treasury Department official in the Reagan and Bush administrations)

Stevenson, <u>The New York Times</u>, 12/01/99

"'...It was great, and I'm a lifelong Democrat,' said Carmela Brown, 60, a former treasurer of the Iowa Democratic Party and local hospital executive. 'He hit on every single tax that is discouraging to Americans...Who can resist a message of a more sensible tax scheme?'"

Gillman, <u>Dallas Morning News</u>, 12/02/99

"Bush...framed his proposal as an effort to grease the wheels of social mobility and provide relief to low-income families, and single mothers groping for the next highest rung on the economic ladder."

Bruni and Stevenson, <u>The New York Times</u>, 12/02/99

6

Defense:
A Period of Consequences

The Citadel
Charleston, South Carolina

September 23, 1999

It is good to be with you. The Citadel is a place of pride and tradition. A place where standards are high and discipline is strong and leaders are born. The men, and now women, of this institution represent a spirit of honor and accomplishment. And I am proud to be with you.

This is a special place to talk about the future of our military, because many of you will shape it. These are times of change and challenge. But you will always return to the values you learned here.

Three months ago, in Providence, Rhode Island, a man rose to take the oath of American citizenship. He was one of many – but his case was different. His name is Sergei Khruschev, a former weapons scientist – and son of the Soviet leader. Sometimes history's great epochs are summed up in small events. The threat of the Cold War was captured in Nikita Khruschev's vow to America, "We will bury you." The story closes, in this final footnote to that age, with America saying to his own son, "We welcome you."

It is a reminder of what this country and its allies have accom-

plished in a century of struggle. Young Americans in uniform –
today's veterans – wrote history with the bold strokes of their
courage. Their character was tested in death marches and jungle
firefights and desert battles. They left long rows of crosses and
Stars of David, fighting for people they did not know, and a future
they would not see. And, in the end, they won an epic struggle to
save liberty itself.

Those who want to lead America accept two obligations. One
is to use our military power wisely, remembering the costs of war.
The other is to honor our commitments to veterans who have paid
those costs.

Our world, shaped by American courage, power and wisdom,
now echoes with American ideals. We won a victory, not just for a
nation, but for a vision. A vision of freedom and individual dignity – defended by democracy, nurtured by free markets, spread by
information technology, carried to the world by free trade. The
advance of freedom – from Asia to Latin America to East and
Central Europe – is creating the conditions for peace.

For America, this is a time of unrivaled military power, economic promise, and cultural influence. It is, in Franklin Roosevelt's
phrase, "the peace of overwhelming victory."

Now a new generation of American leaders will determine how
that power and influence are used – a generation after the hard but
clear struggle against an evil empire. Our challenge is not as obvious, but just as noble: To turn these years of influence into decades
of peace.

But peace is not ordained, it is earned. It is not a harbor
where we rest, it is a voyage we must chart. Even in this time of
hope and confidence, we can see the signs of uncertainty.

We see the contagious spread of missile technology and
weapons of mass destruction. We know that this era of American
preeminence is also an era of car bombers and plutonium mer-
chants and cyber terrorists and drug cartels and unbalanced dicta-

tors – all the unconventional and invisible threats of new technologies and old hatreds. These challenges can be overcome, but they can not be ignored.

Building a durable peace will require strong alliances, expanding trade and confident diplomacy. It will require tough realism in our dealings with China and Russia. It will require firmness with regimes like North Korea and Iraq – regimes that hate our values and resent our success. I will address all these priorities in the future. But I want to begin with the foundation of our peace – a strong, capable and modern military.

The American armed forces have an irreplaceable role in the world. They give confidence to our allies; deter the aggression of our enemies; and allow our nation to shape a stable peace. The common defense is the sworn duty and chief responsibility of a president. And, if elected, I will set three goals: I will renew the bond of trust between the American president and the American military. I will defend the American people against missiles and terror. And I will begin creating the military of the next century.

Our military is without peer, but it is not without problems.

The men and women of our armed forces stand in the best tradition of the citizen soldier, who for two centuries has kept our country safe and free. All are volunteers – active, Reserve and Guard – who willingly accept the burdens and dangers of service.

Volunteers who demonstrate the highest form of citizenship.

I have great faith in those who serve our nation – in the temper of their will and the quality of their spirit. These are men and women who love their country more than their comfort. Men and women who have never failed us, wherever there is honor to be earned, or interests defended. But even the highest morale is eventually undermined by back-to-back deployments, poor pay, shortages of spare parts and equipment, and rapidly declining readiness.

Not since the years before Pearl Harbor has our investment in national defense been so low as a percentage of GNP. Yet rarely has our military been so freely used – an average of one deployment every nine weeks in the last few years. Since the end of the Cold War, our ground forces have been deployed more frequently, while our defense budget has fallen by nearly 40 percent.

Something has to give, and it's giving. Resources are overstretched. Frustration is up, as families are separated and strained. Morale is down. Recruitment is more difficult. And many of our best people in the military are headed for civilian life. In 1998, the Air Force missed its reenlistment goals for the first time since 1981. Army recruiting is at a 20 year low.

Consider a few facts: Thousands of members of the armed forces are on food stamps. Last year, more than $21 million worth of WIC vouchers – the Women, Infants and Children program – were redeemed at military commissaries. Many others in uniform get Army Emergency Relief or depend on their parents.

This is not the way that a great nation should reward courage and idealism. It is ungrateful, it is unwise and it is unacceptable.

This Administration wants things both ways: To command great forces, without supporting them. To launch today's new causes, with little thought of tomorrow's consequences.

A volunteer military has only two paths. It can lower its standards to fill its ranks. Or it can inspire the best and brightest to join and stay.

This starts with better pay, better treatment and better training. Recently, after years of neglect, a significant pay raise was finally passed. My first budget will go further – adding a billion dollars in salary increases. We also will provide targeted bonuses for those with special skills. Two-thirds of military family housing units are now substandard, and they must be renovated. And we must improve the quality of training at our bases and national training centers. Shortfalls on the proving ground become disasters on the battlefield.

But our military requires more than good treatment. It needs the rallying point of a defining mission. And that mission is to deter wars – and win wars when deterrence fails. Sending our military on vague, aimless and endless deployments is the swift solvent of morale.

As president, I will order an immediate review of our overseas deployments – in dozens of countries. The longstanding commitments we have made to our allies are the strong foundation of our current peace. I will keep these pledges to defend friends from aggression. The problem comes with open-ended deployments and unclear military missions. In these cases we will ask, "What is our goal, can it be met, and when do we leave?" As I've said before, I will work hard to find political solutions that allow an orderly and timely withdrawal from places like Kosovo and Bosnia. We will encourage our allies to take a broader role. We will not be hasty. But we will not be permanent peacekeepers, dividing warring parties. This is not our strength or our calling.

America will not retreat from the world. On the contrary, I will replace diffuse commitments with focused ones. I will replace uncertain missions with well-defined objectives. This will preserve the resources of American power and public will. The presence of American forces overseas is one of the most profound symbols of our commitment to allies and friends. And our allies know that if America is committed everywhere, our commitments are everywhere suspect. We must be selective in the use of our military, precisely because America has other great responsibilities that cannot be slighted or compromised. And this review of our deployments will also reduce the tension on an overstretched military. Nothing would be better for morale than clarity and focus from the commander-in-chief.

My second goal is to build America's defenses on the troubled frontiers of technology and terror. The protection of America itself will assume a high priority in a new century. Once a strategic afterthought, homeland defense has become an urgent duty.

For most of our history, America felt safe behind two great oceans. But with the spread of technology, distance no longer means security. North Korea is proving that even a poor and backward country, in the hands of a tyrant, can reach across oceans to threaten us. It has developed missiles capable of hitting Hawaii and Alaska. Iran has made rapid strides in its missile program, and Iraq persists in a race to do the same. In 1996, after some tension over Taiwan, a Chinese general reminded America that China possesses the means to incinerate Los Angeles with nuclear missiles.

Add to this the threat of biological, chemical and nuclear terrorism – barbarism emboldened by technology. These weapons can be delivered, not just by ballistic missiles, but by everything from airplanes to cruise missiles, from shipping containers to suitcases. And consider the prospect of information warfare, in which hacker terrorists may try to disrupt finance, communication, transportation and public health.

Let me be clear. Our first line of defense is a simple message: Every group or nation must know, if they sponsor such attacks, our response will be devastating.

But we must do more. At the earliest possible date, my administration will deploy anti-ballistic missile systems, both theater and national, to guard against attack and blackmail. To make this possible, we will offer Russia the necessary amendments to the anti-ballistic missile treaty – an artifact of Cold War confrontation. Both sides know that we live in a different world from 1972, when that treaty was signed. If Russia refuses the changes we propose, we will give prompt notice, under the provisions of the treaty, that we can no longer be a party to it. I will have a solemn obligation to protect the American people and our allies, not to protect arms control agreements signed almost 30 years ago.

We will defend the American homeland by strengthening our intelligence community – focusing on human intelligence and the early detection of terrorist operations both here and abroad. And when direct threats to America are discovered, I know that the best defense can be a strong and swift offense – including the use of Special Operations Forces and long-range strike capabilities.

And there is more to be done preparing here at home. I will put a high priority on detecting and responding to terrorism on our soil. The federal government must take this threat seriously – working closely with researchers and industry to increase surveillance and develop treatments for chemical and biological agents.

But defending our nation is just the beginning of our challenge. My third goal is to take advantage of a tremendous opportunity – given few nations in history – to extend the current peace into the far realm of the future. A chance to project America's peaceful influence, not just across the world, but across the years.

This opportunity is created by a revolution in the technology of war. Power is increasingly defined, not by mass or size, but by mobility and swiftness. Influence is measured in information, safety is gained in stealth, and force is projected on the long arc of precision-guided weapons. This revolution perfectly matches the strengths of our country – the skill of our people and the superiority of our technology. The best way to keep the peace is to redefine war on our terms.

Yet today our military is still organized more for Cold War threats than for the challenges of a new century – for industrial age operations, rather than for information age battles. There is almost no relationship between our budget priorities and a strategic vision. The last seven years have been wasted in inertia and idle talk. Now we must shape the future with new concepts, new strategies, new resolve.

In the late 1930s, as Britain refused to adapt to the new realities of war, Winston Churchill observed, "The era of procrastination, of half-measures, of soothing and baffling expedients, of delays, is coming to a close. In its place we are entering a period of consequences."

Our military and our nation are entering another period of consequences – a time of rapid change and momentous choices.

As president, I will begin an immediate, comprehensive review of our military – the structure of its forces, the state of its strategy, the priorities of its procurement – conducted by a leadership team under the Secretary of Defense. I will give the Secretary a broad mandate – to challenge the status quo and envision a new architecture of American defense for decades to come. We will modernize some existing weapons and equipment, necessary for current tasks. But our relative peace allows us to do this selectively. The real goal is to move beyond marginal improvements – to replace existing programs with new technologies and strategies. To use this window of opportunity to skip a generation of technology. This will require spending more – and spending more wisely.

We know that power, in the future, will be projected in different ways.

The Gulf War was a stunning victory. But it took six months of planning and transport to summon our fleets and divisions and position them for battle.

In the future, we are unlikely to have that kind of time. Enemy ballistic and cruise missiles and weapons of mass destruction may make such operations difficult. Satellite technology, commercially available, may reveal to potential enemies the location of our ships and troops. We may not have months to transport massive divisions to waiting bases, or to build new infrastructure on site.

Our forces in the next century must be agile, lethal, readily deployable, and require a minimum of logistical support. We must be able to project our power over long distances, in days or weeks rather than months. Our military must be able to identify targets by a variety of means – from a Marine patrol to a satellite. Then be able to destroy those targets almost instantly, with an array of weapons, from a submarine-launched cruise missile, to mobile long-range artillery.

On land, our heavy forces must be lighter. Our light forces must be more lethal. All must be easier to deploy. And these forces must be organized in smaller, more agile formations, rather than cumbersome divisions.

On the seas, we need to pursue promising ideas like the arsenal ship – a stealthy ship packed with long-range missiles to destroy targets from great distances.

In the air, we must be able to strike from across the world with pinpoint accuracy – with long-range aircraft and perhaps with unmanned systems.

In space, we must be able to protect our network of satellites, essential to the flow of our commerce and the defense of our country.

All this will require a new spirit of innovation. Many officers have expressed their impatience with a widespread, bureaucratic mindset that frustrates creativity. I will encourage a culture of command where change is welcomed and rewarded, not dreaded. I will ensure that visionary leaders who take risks are recognized and promoted.

When our comprehensive review is complete, I will expect the military's budget priorities to match our strategic vision – not the particular visions of the services, but a joint vision for change. I will earmark at least 20 percent of the procurement budget for acquisition programs that propel America generations ahead in military technology. And I will direct the Secretary of Defense to allocate these funds to the services that prove most effective in developing new programs that do so. I intend to force new thinking and hard choices.

The transformation of our military will require a new and greater emphasis on research and development. So I will also commit an additional $20 billion to defense R&D between the time I take office and 2006.

Even if I am elected, I will not command the new military we create. That will be left to a president who comes after me. The results of our effort will not be seen for many years. The outcome of great battles is often determined by decisions on funding and technology made decades before, in the quiet days of peace. But these choices on spending and strategy either support the young men and women who must fight the future's wars – or betray their lives and squander their valor.

I am under no illusions. I know that transforming our military is a massive undertaking. When President Lincoln was attempting to organize his army, he compared the job to bailing out the Potomac River with a teaspoon. What I propose will be impossible without allies – both in the military and in the Congress.

To the military I say: We intend to change your structure, but we will respect your culture. Our military culture was formed by generations of trial and tradition – codes and loyalties born of two centuries' worth of experience.

For the changes I seek, I will count on these codes and loyalties. I will count on a culture that prizes duty, welcomes clear orders, accepts sacrifice, and is devoted above all to the defense of the United States.

I will count on these values, because I will challenge our military to reform itself in fundamental ways.

To the Congress I say: Join me in creating a new strategic vision for our military – a set of goals that will take precedence over the narrow interests of states and regions. I will reach out to reform-minded members of Congress, particularly to overturn laws and regulations that discourage outsourcing and undermine efficiency. Our military must embrace the productivity revolution that has transformed American business. And once a new strategy is clear, I will confront the Congress when it uses the defense budget as a source of pork or patronage.

Moments of national opportunity are either seized or lost, and the consequences reach across decades. Our opportunity is here –

to show that a new generation can renew America's purpose.

I know this is a world of hard choices and new tasks. A world of terror and missiles and madmen. A world requiring, not just might, but wisdom.

But my generation is fortunate. In the world of our fathers, we have seen how America should conduct itself. We have seen leaders who fought a world war and organized the peace. We have seen power exercised without swagger and influence displayed without bluster. We have seen the modesty of true strength, the humility of real greatness. We have seen American power tempered by American character. And I have seen all of this personally and closely and clearly.

Now comes our time of testing. Our measure is taken, not only by what we have and use, but what we build and leave behind. And nothing this generation could ever build will matter more than the means to defend our nation and extend our peace.

Position Paper
Defense: A Period of Consequences

"Today our military is still organized more for Cold War threats than for the challenges of a new century... There is almost no relationship between our budget priorities and a strategic vision. The last seven years have been wasted in inertia and idle talk. Now we must shape the future with new concepts, new strategies, new resolve... We are entering 'a period of consequences.'"

Governor George W. Bush

EXECUTIVE SUMMARY

Governor Bush believes that a strong, capable and modern military is essential to defend our nation, advance U.S. interests, and extend our peace. As President, he will set three goals for our nation's defense:

To Renew the Bond of Trust Between the President and the Military, Governor Bush will:

- Respect the military's tradition and culture, while changing its structure.

- Increase by $1 billion the currently planned military pay raise to encourage the best and brightest to enlist – and reenlist – in the armed forces.

- Renovate substandard military housing and improve military training.

- Maintain longstanding U.S. commitments, but order an immediate review of overseas deployments in dozens of countries, with the aim of replacing uncertain missions with well-defined objectives.

To Defend the American Homeland, Governor Bush will:

- Deter terrorist attacks by ensuring every group or nation understands if they sponsor attacks, the U.S. response will be devastating.

- Deploy both national and theater anti-ballistic missile defenses, as soon as possible.

- Amend the ABM Treaty, or, if Russia fails to agree, withdraw from it.

- Strengthen our intelligence community's ability to detect terrorist threats, and develop long-range strike capabilities to eliminate such threats before they arise.

- Promote cooperation with our allies, who should share the burden of defense.

To Begin to Create the Military of the Future, Governor Bush will:

- Order a comprehensive military review to develop a new architecture for American defense designed to meet the challenges of the next century.

- Seize the opportunity to skip a generation of weapons, not merely improving existing systems, but replacing them with a new generation of technology: land forces that are lighter but more lethal, air power – manned or unmanned – that can accurately strike across long distances, and naval power that packs a bigger punch in smaller platforms.

- Encourage a spirit of innovation and experimentation within the military.

- Earmark at least 20 percent of the procurement budget for acquisition programs that propel America generations ahead in military technology.

- Increase defense R&D spending by at least $20 billion from FY2002 to FY2006.

The State of Our Armed Forces: Overextended and Unprepared for the Future

Governor Bush believes a strong, capable, modern military is the foundation of the peace we enjoy today and hope to extend for future generations. Unfortunately, the Clinton-Gore Administration has presided over a debilitating mix of increased troop deployments and decreased defense spending:

- Since the end of the Cold War, overseas deployments of U.S. troops have increased dramatically. During the Clinton-Gore Administration, our military has undertaken an average of one new deployment every nine weeks.

- In the same period, U.S. defense spending has declined by nearly 40 percent. It is now at its lowest level as a percentage of GNP than at any time since 1940. This has led to what the Administration's own Under Secretary of Defense has called a budgetary "death spiral" – pouring more and more money into older and older equipment, draining funds from modernization.

Thus, U.S. forces are overused and underfunded precisely when they are confronted by a host of new threats and challenges: the spread of weapons of mass destruction, the rise of cyberterrorism, the proliferation of missile technology. The result is damaged morale, and a military force unprepared to deal with the threats of a new century.

Governor Bush believes that America's military is faced with a moment of opportunity – an opportunity to transform itself, and thus ensure peace for generations. Seizing this opportunity will require more spending, but equally as important, spending more wisely. The right choices must be made to repair morale, protect America, and create a military capable of meeting the challenges of the 21st Century. Thus, as President, Governor Bush will:

- Renew the bond of trust between the President and the military by increasing pay, improving housing, and insisting that deployments have well-defined objectives;

- Defend the American people against missiles and terrorists; and

- Begin to create the military of the future – lethal, agile, easier to deploy – by capitalizing on new technologies.

In implementing these goals, Governor Bush will challenge the military to transform itself. He will respect the military's tradition and culture, while changing its structure and encouraging a spirit of innovation.

Goal #1. Renew the Bond of Trust Between the President and the Military

The current Administration's combination of frequent but unfocused deployments and insufficient resources has led to lower morale and declining enlistment and reenlistment. Indeed, no aspect of the current neglect of the nation's armed forces is more worrisome than the effect on the men and women in uniform – and their families – who are forced to accept low pay and inadequate housing:

- The overall gap between civilian and military pay stands at more than 13 percent.

- According to the most recent survey, almost 12,000 members of the armed forces have been forced to rely on food stamps; others receive Women, Infants and Children funding or Army Emergency Relief – or depend on their parents.

- One-third of military families are housed in approximately 320,000 units, 66 percent of which are substandard, according to the Chairman of the Joint Chiefs of Staff.

In addition to dealing with low pay and poor housing, the men and women of the military are frequently subjected to deployments that are too often open-ended and lacking in clear objectives. This has produced serious morale problems that have triggered a growing crisis in retention and a shortage of skilled personnel.

As President, Governor Bush will renew the bond of trust between the Oval Office and America's men and women in uniform. Much as Ronald Reagan restored the attraction of military life for individuals and families.

Governor Bush will focus on making the military a magnet for the best and brightest in America and as President, he will:

Increase by $1 Billion the Planned Military Pay Raise: In a Bush Administration, military pay will be increased by $1 billion – or an average of about $750 per active duty service member – over and above the pay increase recently passed by Congress. These additional funds will help narrow the overall difference in compensation between the armed forces and the civilian sector. Governor Bush will also increase targeted reenlistment bonuses and special pay for critical specialties. This will further reduce the pay gap for individuals with skills in high demand, such as pilots, computer programmers, and engineers.

Improve Military Housing: As President, Governor Bush will work with Congress to ensure that service members and their families no longer have to tolerate substandard housing. In some cases, this will involve renovation or construction of barracks or family housing units. In other cases, it will mean increasing basic housing allowances, especially in high cost areas.

Improve Military Training: Despite recent increases, unfunded requirements remain in training center facilities, equipment and operations. As President, Governor Bush will work with Congress to ensure that such shortfalls are addressed and the decline in the quality and level of training of our men and women in uniform is reversed.

Order an Immediate Review of Overseas Deployments: As President, Governor Bush will pledge to maintain longstanding commitments, but will order a review of other overseas deployments. To improve morale and preserve resources for important interests, diffuse commitments will be replaced with focused ones. National security planners will scrutinize open-ended deployments, reassess U.S. goals, and ascertain whether they can be met. For example, as he has previously stated, he will work hard as President for political solutions that allow an orderly and timely withdrawal from places like Kosovo and Bosnia.

Goal #2. Defend the American Homeland

The second pillar of Governor Bush's plan for America's defense is to protect America itself from attack. Today, over two dozen countries have ballistic missiles. A number of them – including North Korea, Iran, and Iraq – are developing missiles that may ultimately reach intercontinental range. Given this new reality, the U.S. government can no longer afford to drag its feet on building and deploying a missile defense system; nor can it continue to allow Cold War arms control agreements to restrict America's ability to defend itself and its allies.

Governor Bush also understands that the defense of our homeland involves much more than protection against missiles. A Congressionally appointed blue-ribbon commission recently concluded that the United States is unprepared to counter the rampant proliferation of nuclear, chemical, and biological weapons around the world. More important, the United States remains vulnerable to a state or terrorist group using those weapons.

To improve the nation's security against missile attack and bolster America's homeland defense, Governor Bush will:

Deter Attacks Against the United States: As President, Governor Bush will deter terrorist attacks by ensuring that every group or nation understands that if they sponsor such attacks, America's response will be devastating.

Deploy Ballistic Missile Defenses: Governor Bush will accelerate research on, and deployment of, both national and theater missile defenses, as soon as possible.

Amend the ABM Treaty, or Withdraw From It: The United States should offer Russia necessary amendments to the Cold War-era Anti-Ballistic Missile (ABM) Treaty to permit deployment of effective national and theater missile defenses. If Russia refuses those changes, the United States should give prompt notice, under the treaty, that we will withdraw from it.

Strengthen U.S. Intelligence Capabilities: As President, Governor Bush will make it a priority to strengthen U.S. intelligence resources, focusing on human intelligence and the early detection of threats to the homeland. Once such threats are detected, the best defense will be a good offense, including the use of Special Operations Forces and long-range strike capabilities.

Improve Cooperation with U.S. Allies: To counter emerging threats, the United States will need improved cooperation with its allies. They face many of the same threats as the United States, and should share in the burden of defense.

Goal #3. Begin Creating the Military of the Future

The third part of Governor Bush's plan for the nation's defense is to use the present window of relative peace to skip a generation of weapons systems and strategies. Today our military is still organized more for Cold War threats than for the challenges of a new century. What is needed is a new architecture for American defense – an architecture that will permit the U.S. to project power swiftly under new conditions. As in the past, the United States will need modern and well-trained forces, sufficient in size to project power rapidly to key regions of the world. Yet, the need to project power will require very different kinds of forces from those in the past:

- First, in the future, adversaries with access to ballistic and cruise missiles, weapons of mass destruction, and other technologies will attempt to deny the United States the enormous advantages of its forward bases and logistics capabilities.

- Second, enemy tactics against American forces will likely be directed at the weakest links in our extension of power. Airfields and ports critical to the flow of American forces and materiel will be targeted.

- Third, the enemy might choose environments in which to fight where American forces that depend on large amounts of logistical support will be at a disadvantage.

To meet such future challenges, Governor Bush believes that our military must develop the capability for very different sorts of forces for power projection. Therefore, as President, Governor Bush will:

Order a Review of U.S. Military Force Structure, Strategy, and Procurement: The review will be conducted by a leadership team under the Secretary of Defense that Governor Bush will charge with creating the military of the future – lethal, agile, easier to deploy. While some existing weapons will need to be modernized, the larger goal will be to skip a generation of technology, replacing existing systems with new technologies and strategies:

- Land Forces. On land, U.S. heavy armored forces must be lighter, and light forces must be made more lethal; all must be easier to deploy.

- Naval Forces. On the seas, U.S. carriers must be complemented by capable smaller platforms. That is why Governor Bush will pursue promising ideas such as the arsenal ship – a stealthy ship loaded with long-range missiles able to destroy targets accurately from great distances.

- Air Power. In the air, a larger portion of the force of the future must be able to strike from across the world with pinpoint accuracy using long-range aircraft – both manned and unmanned. Thus, as President, Governor Bush will order a review of the entire U.S. aircraft program, encompassing not only ongoing shorter-range fighter programs, but also bomber and support aircraft needs.

- Space and Information Systems. The military of tomorrow must also be as adept at operating in space and the information environment as it has been on land, sea, and in the air. Space-based assets will aid in projecting power and protecting the homeland. In addition, America must be prepared not only to defend its vulnerable infrastructure against cyber attacks, but also to develop offensive information warfare capabilities.

Once the comprehensive review is complete, Governor Bush will move aggressively to create the military of the future. Specifically, he will:

Earmark at Least 20 Percent of the Procurement Budget to Address Future

<u>Challenges</u>: The military's budget priorities must match the new strategic vision. As President, Governor Bush will direct the Secretary of Defense to earmark at least 20 percent of the total procurement budget for acquisition programs that propel America generations ahead in military technology. To promote needed inter-service cooperation and reduce costly redundancy, the Secretary of Defense, not individual services, will set the spending priorities.

<u>Encourage a Spirit of Innovation</u>: Developing and leading the military of the future will require a new spirit of innovation. Thus, as President, Governor Bush will encourage a culture of command, and ensure that visionary leaders are recognized and promoted.

<u>Increase Defense R&D Spending by at Least $20 Billion</u>: Transforming the military and realizing the promise of new technology, will require a substantially greater emphasis on research and development. Thus, R&D spending will be increased by at least $20 billion from FY2002 to FY2006. Furthermore, to promote a culture of innovation, the military will be strongly encouraged to "wildcat" – to try various methods and technologies to solve operational problems. Military commanders and service chiefs will be judged on how well they experiment to meet the new operational challenges envisioned in the future.

<u>Ask Congress to Join in Creating a New Strategic Vision</u>: As President, Governor Bush will reach out to reform-minded members of Congress. He will also confront Congress when it uses the defense budget as a source of pork or patronage.

What Others Say

*"A serious setting – The Citadel. A serious subject – U.S. defense policy…
In the third in a series of policy speeches, the Governor outlined a…plan for
[a] more potent, more mobile weaponry, a better-paid military, and a better-
protected America. The plan includes deployment of anti-ballistic missile
systems…mixing his presidential vision of defense policy in the next century
with a critique of policy in this decade…Criticizing what he called vague,
aimless and endless deployments, Bush promised a comprehensive review
of U.S. military missions abroad."*

Candy Crowley, CNN, 9/23/99

*"There were shades of former President Ronald Reagan's thinking and oratory
in the way Bush summoned the specter of foreign evils – 'a world of terror and
missiles and madmen,' he said – and emphasized American technological
prowess as the amulet against them."*

Frank Bruni, The New York Times, 9/24/99

*"George W. Bush…proposed an ambitious rebuilding of the military to safe-
guard American interests in a world still full of risks."*

Michael Kranish, Boston Globe, 9/24/99

*"Governor George W. Bush of Texas Thursday proposed sweeping changes in
the armed forces, proposing that some weapons under development should be
scrapped in favor of futuristic ones, and that massive land forces must become
'smaller, more agile formations.'…[he] detailed…what he would do as
commander-in-chief…"*

Rowan Scarborough, Washington Times, 9/24/99

What Others Say

"The role of the U.S. Army is so essential to national security that it deserves to be debated by the presidential candidates. So far, only one – George W. Bush – has said anything significant…. It will take civilian leadership to shake up the Army. The Clinton administration has provided very little. Of the current presidential candidates, only George W. Bush has called for radical reforms of the armed forces. He sensibly proposed that the Army stop building World War II-era weapons like heavy tanks and instead call a timeout: take advantage of America's current military supremacy to pause, 'skip a generation' of technology and invest in futuristic high-tech systems that can be quickly deployed. (Bush's lead challenger, John McCain, and the two Democratic rivals, Al Gore and Bill Bradley, have said almost nothing.) [Former Army Chief of Staff General Dennis] Reimer, the veteran of endless bureaucratic struggles, welcomed Bush's indictment of the status quo. 'Great,' he told Newsweek. 'Maybe that will provoke the debate this country needs to have about the future of its military.'"

John Barry and Evan Thomas, "Not Your Father's Army,"
Newsweek, 11/22/99

"In his speech last week on national defense and foreign policy, Texas Gov. George W. Bush, the front-runner for the Republican presidential nomination, left no doubt where he stood on what is arguably the most important issue that the White House's next occupant will face early next century. 'At the earliest possible date,' Mr. Bush clearly declared, 'my administration will deploy anti-ballistic missile systems, both theater and national, to guard against attack and blackmail.'…Demonstrating that his priorities as U.S. commander-in-chief would be in order, Mr. Bush refreshingly added, 'I will have a solemn obligation to protect the American people and our allies, not to protect arms control agreements signed almost 30 years ago.'…"

Editorial, Washington Times, 9/29/99

7

Foreign Policy:
A Distinctly American Internationalism

The Ronald Reagan Presidential Library
Simi Valley, California

November 19, 1999

It is an honor to be with you at the Reagan Library. Thank you Secretary Shultz for your decades of service to America – and for your kindness and counsel over the last several months. And thank you Mrs. Reagan for this invitation – and for your example of loyalty and love and courage.

My wife Laura says that behind every great man there is a surprised woman. But, Mrs. Reagan, you were never surprised by the greatness of your husband. You believed it from the start. And now the rest of the world sees him as you always have – as a hero in the American story. A story in which a single individual can shape history. A story in which evil is real, but courage and decency triumph.

We live in the nation President Reagan restored, and the world he helped to save. A world of nations reunited and tyrants humbled. A world of prisoners released and exiles come home. And today there is a prayer shared by free people everywhere: God bless you, Ronald Reagan.

Two months ago, at the Citadel in South Carolina, I talked

about American defense. This must be the first focus of a president, because it is his first duty to the Constitution. Even in this time of pride and promise, America has determined enemies, who hate our values and resent our success – terrorists and crime syndicates and drug cartels and unbalanced dictators. The Empire has passed, but evil remains.

We must protect our homeland and our allies against missiles and terror and blackmail.

We must restore the morale of our military – squandered by shrinking resources and multiplying missions – with better training, better treatment and better pay.

And we must master the new technology of war – to extend our peaceful influence, not just across the world, but across the years.

In the defense of our nation, a president must be a clear-eyed realist. There are limits to the smiles and scowls of diplomacy. Armies and missiles are not stopped by stiff notes of condemnation. They are held in check by strength and purpose and the promise of swift punishment.

But there is more to say, because military power is not the final measure of might. Our realism must make a place for the human spirit.

This spirit, in our time, has caused dictators to fear and empires to fall. And it has left an honor roll of courage and idealism: Scharansky, Havel, Walesa, Mandela. The most powerful force in the world is not a weapon or a nation but a truth: that we are spiritual beings, and that freedom is "the soul's right to breathe."

In the dark days of 1941 – the low point of our modern epic – there were about a dozen democracies left on the planet. Entering a new century, there are nearly 120. There is a direction in events, a current in our times. "Depend on it," said Edmund Burke. "The lovers of freedom will be free."

America cherishes that freedom, but we do not own it. We value the elegant structures of our own democracy – but realize that, in other societies, the architecture will vary. We propose our principles, we must not impose our culture.

Yet the basic principles of human freedom and dignity are universal. People should be able to say what they think. Worship as they wish. Elect those who govern them. These ideals have proven their power on every continent. In former colonies – and the nations that ruled them. Among the allies of World War II – and the countries they vanquished. And these ideals are equally valid north of the 38th parallel. They are just as true in the Pearl River Delta. They remain true 90 miles from our shores, on an island prison, ruled by a revolutionary relic.

Some have tried to pose a choice between American ideals and American interests – between who we are and how we act. But the choice is false. America, by decision and destiny, promotes political freedom – and gains the most when democracy advances. America believes in free markets and free trade – and benefits most when markets are opened. America is a peaceful power – and gains the greatest dividend from democratic stability. Precisely because we have no territorial objectives, our gains are not measured in the losses of others. They are counted in the conflicts we avert, the prosperity we share and the peace we extend.

Sometimes this balance takes time to achieve – and requires us to deal with nations that do not share our values. Sometimes the defenders of freedom must show patience as well as resolution. But that patience comes of confidence, not compromise. We believe, with George Washington, that "Liberty, when it begins to take root, is a plant of rapid growth." And we firmly believe our nation is on the right side of history – the side of man's dignity and God's justice.

Few nations have been given the advantages and opportunities of our own. Few have been more powerful as a country, or more successful as a cause. But there are risks, even for the powerful. "I have many reasons to be optimistic," said Pericles in the golden age of Athens. "Indeed, I am more afraid of our own blunders than of the enemy's devices."

America's first temptation is withdrawal – to build a proud tower of protectionism and isolation.

In a world that depends on America to reconcile old rivals and balance ancient ambitions, this is the shortcut to chaos. It is an approach that abandons our allies, and our ideals. The vacuum left by America's retreat would invite challenges to our power. And the result, in the long run, would be a stagnant America and a savage world.

American foreign policy cannot be founded on fear. Fear that American workers can't compete. Fear that America will corrupt the world – or be corrupted by it. This fear has no place in the party of Reagan, or in the party of Truman. In times of peril, our nation did not shrink from leadership. At this moment of opportunity, I have no intention of betraying American interests, American obligations and American honor.

America's second temptation is drift – for our nation to move from crisis to crisis like a cork in a current.

Unless a president sets his own priorities, his priorities will be set by others – by adversaries, or the crisis of the moment, live on CNN. American policy can become random and reactive – untethered to the interests of our country.

America must be involved in the world. But that does not mean our military is the answer to every difficult foreign policy situation – a substitute for strategy. American internationalism should not mean action without vision, activity without priority, and missions without end – an approach that squanders American will and drains American energy.

American foreign policy must be more than the management of crisis. It must have a great and guiding goal: to turn this time of American influence into generations of democratic peace.

This is accomplished by concentrating on enduring national

interests. And these are my priorities. An American president should work with our strong democratic allies in Europe and Asia to extend the peace. He should promote a fully democratic Western Hemisphere, bound together by free trade. He should defend America's interests in the Persian Gulf and advance peace in the Middle East, based upon a secure Israel. He must check the contagious spread of weapons of mass destruction, and the means to deliver them. He must lead toward a world that trades in freedom. And he must pursue all these goals with focus, patience and strength.

I will address these responsibilities as this campaign continues. To each, I bring the same approach: A distinctly American internationalism. Idealism, without illusions. Confidence, without conceit. Realism, in the service of American ideals.

Today I want to talk about Europe and Asia...the world's strategic heartland...our greatest priority. Home of long-time allies, and looming rivals. Behind the United States, Eurasia has the next six largest economies. The next six largest military budgets.

The Eurasian landmass, in our century, has seen the indignities of colonialism and the excesses of nationalism. Its people have been sacrificed to brutal wars and totalitarian ambitions. America has discovered, again and again, that our history is inseparable from their tragedy. And we are rediscovering that our interests are served by their success.

In this immense region, we are guided, not by an ambition, but by a vision. A vision in which no great power, or coalition of great powers, dominates or endangers our friends. In which America encourages stability from a position of strength. A vision in which people and capital and information can move freely, creating bonds of progress, ties of culture and momentum toward democracy.

This is different from the trumpet call of the Cold War. We are no longer fighting a great enemy, we are asserting a great principle: that the talents and dreams of average people – their warm human hopes and loves – should be rewarded by freedom and protected by peace. We are defending the nobility of normal lives, lived in obedience to God and conscience, not to government.

The challenge comes because two of Eurasia's greatest powers – China and Russia – are powers in transition. And it is difficult to know their intentions when they do not know their own futures. If they become America's friends, that friendship will steady the world. But if not, the peace we seek may not be found.

China, in particular, has taken different shapes in different eyes at different times. An empire to be divided. A door to be opened. A model of collective conformity. A diplomatic card to be played. One year, it is said to be run by "the butchers of Beijing." A few years later, the same administration pronounces it a "strategic partner."

We must see China clearly – not through the filters of posturing and partisanship. China is rising, and that is inevitable. Here, our interests are plain: We welcome a free and prosperous China. We predict no conflict. We intend no threat. And there are areas where we must try to cooperate: preventing the spread of weapons of mass destruction...attaining peace on the Korean peninsula.

Yet the conduct of China's government can be alarming abroad, and appalling at home. Beijing has been investing its growing wealth in strategic nuclear weapons...new ballistic missiles...a blue-water navy and a long-range airforce. It is an espionage threat to our country. Meanwhile, the State Department has reported that "all public dissent against the party and government [has been] effectively silenced" – a tragic achievement in a nation of 1.2 billion people. China's government is an enemy of religious freedom and a sponsor of forced abortion – policies without reason and without mercy.

All of these facts must be squarely faced. China is a competitor, not a strategic partner. We must deal with China without ill-will – but without illusions.

By the same token, that regime must have no illusions about American power and purpose. As Dean Rusk observed during the Cold War, "It is not healthy for a regime...to incur, by their lawlessness and aggressive conduct, the implacable opposition of the American people."

We must show American power and purpose in strong support for our Asian friends and allies – for democratic South Korea across the Yellow Sea...for democratic Japan and the Philippines across the China seas...for democratic Australia and Thailand. This means keeping our pledge to deter aggression against the Republic of Korea, and strengthening security ties with Japan. This means expanding theater missile defenses among our allies.

And this means honoring our promises to the people of Taiwan. We do not deny there is one China. But we deny the right of Beijing to impose its rule on a free people. As I've said before, we will help Taiwan to defend itself.

The greatest threats to peace come when democratic forces are weak and disunited. Right now, America has many important bilateral alliances in Asia. We should work toward a day when the fellowship of free Pacific nations is as strong and united as our Atlantic Partnership. If I am president, China will find itself respected as a great power, but in a region of strong democratic alliances. It will be unthreatened, but not unchecked.

China will find in America a confident and willing trade partner. And with trade comes our standing invitation into the world of economic freedom. China's entry into the World Trade Organization is welcome, and this should open the door for Taiwan as well. But given China's poor record in honoring agreements, it will take a strong administration to hold them to their word.

If I am president, China will know that America's values are always part of America's agenda. Our advocacy of human freedom is not a formality of diplomacy, it is a fundamental commitment of our country. It is the source of our confidence that communism, in

155

every form, has seen its day.

And I view free trade as an important ally in what Ronald Reagan called "a forward strategy for freedom." The case for trade is not just monetary, but moral. Economic freedom creates habits of liberty. And habits of liberty create expectations of democracy. There are no guarantees, but there are good examples, from Chile to Taiwan. Trade freely with China, and time is on our side.

Russia stands as another reminder that a world increasingly at peace is also a world in transition. Here, too, patience is needed – patience, consistency, and a principled reliance on democratic forces.

In the breadth of its land, the talent and courage of its people, the wealth of its resources, and the reach of its weapons, Russia is a great power, and must always be treated as such. Few people have suffered more in this century. And though we trust the worst is behind them, their troubles are not over. This past decade, for Russia, has been an epic of deliverance and disappointment.

Our first order of business is the national security of our nation – and here both Russia and the United States face a changed world. Instead of confronting each other, we confront the legacy of a dead ideological rivalry – thousands of nuclear weapons, which, in the case of Russia, may not be secure. And together we also face an emerging threat – from rogue nations, nuclear theft and accidental launch. All this requires nothing short of a new strategic relationship to protect the peace of the world.

We can hope that the new Russian Duma will ratify START II, as we have done. But this is not our most pressing challenge. The greater problem was first addressed in 1991 by Senator Lugar and Senator Sam Nunn. In an act of foresight and statesmanship, they realized that existing Russian nuclear facilities were in danger of being compromised. Under the Nunn-Lugar program, security at many Russian nuclear facilities has been improved and warheads have been destroyed.

Even so, the Energy Department warns us that our estimates of Russian nuclear stockpiles could be off by as much as 30 percent. In other words, a great deal of Russian nuclear material cannot be accounted for. The next president must press for an accurate inventory of all this material. And we must do more. I'll ask the Congress to increase substantially our assistance to dismantle as many of Russia's weapons as possible, as quickly as possible.

We will still, however, need missile defense systems – both theater and national. If I am commander-in-chief, we will develop and deploy them.

Under the mutual threat of rogue nations, there is a real possibility the Russians could join with us and our friends and allies to cooperate on missile defense systems. But there is a condition. Russia must break its dangerous habit of proliferation.

In the hard work of halting proliferation, the Comprehensive Test Ban Treaty is not the answer. I've said that our nation should continue its moratorium on testing. Yet far more important is to constrict the supply of nuclear materials and the means to deliver them – by making this a priority with Russia and China. Our nation must cut off the demand for nuclear weapons – by addressing the security concerns of those who renounce these weapons. And our nation must diminish the evil attraction of these weapons for rogue states – by rendering them useless with missile defense. The Comprehensive Test Ban Treaty does nothing to gain these goals. It does not stop proliferation, especially to renegade regimes. It is not verifiable. It is not enforceable. And it would stop us from ensuring the safety and reliability of our nation's deterrent, should the need arise. On these crucial matters, it offers only words and false hopes and high intentions – with no guarantees whatever. We can fight the spread of nuclear weapons, but we cannot wish them away with unwise treaties.

Dealing with Russia on essential issues will be far easier if we are dealing with a democratic and free Russia. Our goal is to promote, not only the appearance of democracy in Russia, but the structures, spirit, and reality of democracy. This is clearly not done by focusing our aid and attention on a corrupt and favored elite. Real change in Russia – as in China – will come not from above, but from below. From a rising class of entrepreneurs and business people. From new leaders in Russia's regions who will build a new Russian state, where power is shared, not controlled. Our assistance, investments and loans should go directly to the Russian people, not to enrich the bank accounts of corrupt officials.

America should reach out to a new generation of Russians through educational exchanges and programs to support the rule of law and a civil society. And the Russian people, next month, must be given a free and fair choice in their election. We cannot buy reform for Russia, but we can be Russia's ally in self-reform.

Even as we support Russian reform, we cannot excuse Russian brutality. When the Russian government attacks civilians – killing women and children, leaving orphans and refugees – it can no longer expect aid from international lending institutions. The Russian government will discover that it cannot build a stable and unified nation on the ruins of human rights. That it cannot learn the lessons of democracy from the textbook of tyranny. We want to cooperate with Russia on its concern with terrorism, but that is impossible unless Moscow operates with civilized self-restraint.

Just as we do not want Russia to descend into cruelty, we do not want it to return to imperialism. Russia does have interests with its newly independent neighbors. But those interests must be expressed in commerce and diplomacy – not coercion and domination. A return to Russian imperialism would endanger both Russian democracy and the states on Russia's borders. The United States should actively support the nations of the Baltics, the Caucasus and Central Asia, along with Ukraine, by promoting regional peace and economic development, and opening links to the wider world.

Often overlooked in our strategic calculations is that great land that rests at the south of Eurasia. This coming century will see democratic India's arrival as a force in the world. A vast population, before long the world's most populous nation. A changing economy, in which 3 of its 5 wealthiest citizens are software entrepreneurs.

India is now debating its future and its strategic path, and the United States must pay it more attention. We should establish more trade and investment with India as it opens to the world. And we should work with the Indian government, ensuring it is a force for stability and security in Asia. This should not undermine our long-standing relationship with Pakistan, which remains crucial to the peace of the region.

All our goals in Eurasia will depend on America strengthening the alliances that sustain our influence – in Europe and East Asia and the Middle East.

Alliances are not just for crises – summoned into action when the fire bell sounds. They are sustained by contact and trust. The Gulf War coalition, for example, was raised on the foundation of a president's vision and effort and integrity. Never again should an American president spend nine days in China, and not even bother to stop in Tokyo or Seoul or Manila. Never again should an American president fall silent when China criticizes our security ties with Japan.

For NATO to be strong, cohesive and active, the President must give it consistent direction: on the alliance's purpose; on Europe's need to invest more in defense capabilities; and, when necessary, in military conflict.

To be relied upon when they are needed, our allies must be respected when they are not.

We have partners, not satellites. Our goal is a fellowship of strong, not weak, nations. And this requires both more American consultation and more American leadership. The United States needs its European allies, as well as friends in other regions, to help us with security challenges as they arise. For our allies, sharing the enormous opportunities of Eurasia also means sharing the burdens and risks of sustaining the peace. The support of friends allows America to reserve its power and will for the vital interests we share.

Likewise, international organizations can serve the cause of peace. I will never place U.S. troops under U.N. command – but the U.N. can help in weapons inspections, peacekeeping and humanitarian efforts. If I am president, America will pay its dues – but only if the U.N.'s bureaucracy is reformed, and our disproportionate share of its costs is reduced.

There must also be reform of international financial institutions – the World Bank and the IMF. They can be a source of stability in economic crisis. But they should not impose austerity, bailing out bankers while impoverishing a middle class. They should not prop up failed and corrupt financial systems. These organizations should encourage the basics of economic growth and free markets. Spreading the rule of law and wise budget practices. Promoting sound banking laws and accounting rules. Most of all, these institutions themselves must be more transparent and accountable.

All the aims I've described today are important. But they are not imperial. America has never been an empire. We may be the only great power in history that had the chance, and refused – preferring greatness to power and justice to glory.

We are a nation that helped defeat Germany in 1945 – which had launched a war costing 55 million lives. Less than five years later we launched an airlift to save the people of Berlin from starvation and tyranny. And a generation of Germans remember the "raisin bombers" that dropped candy and raisins for children.

We are a nation that defeated Japan – then distributed food, wrote a constitution, encouraged labor unions and gave women the right to vote. Japanese who expected retribution received mercy instead. Over the entrance of one American army camp, there was a banner that read, "Be neat. Be soldierly. Be proud. Behave. Be American."

No one questioned what those words meant: "Be American." They meant we were humble in victory. That we were liberators, not conquerors. And when American soldiers hugged the survivors of death camps, and shared their tears, and welcomed them back from a nightmare world, our country was confirmed in its calling.

The duties of our day are different. But the values of our nation do not change. Let us reject the blinders of isolationism, just as we refuse the crown of empire. Let us not dominate others with our power – or betray them with our indifference. And let us have an American foreign policy that reflects American character. The modesty of true strength. The humility of real greatness.

This is the strong heart of America. And this will be the spirit of my administration.

I believe this kind of foreign policy will inspire our people and restore the bipartisanship so necessary to our peace and security.

Many years ago, Alexander Solzhenitsyn challenged American politicians. "Perhaps," he said, "some of you still feel yourselves just as representatives of your state or party. We do not perceive these differences. We do not look on you as Democrats or Republicans, not as representatives of the East or West Coast or the Midwest....Upon [you] depends whether the course of world history will tend to tragedy or salvation."

That is still our challenge. And that is still our choice.

Foreign Policy: A Distinctly American Internationalism

Governor Bush's Foreign Policy Priorities:

American foreign policy must be more than the management of crisis. It must have a great and guiding goal: to turn this time of American influence into generations of democratic peace. This is accomplished by concentrating on enduring national interests and by resisting the temptation to withdraw from the world: withdrawal would abandon our allies and our ideals.

An American president must set priorities and stick to them to avoid drift in foreign policy.

As President, Governor Bush will:

- Work with our strong democratic allies in Europe and Asia to extend the peace and deal with the challenges of China and Russia - two great powers in transition

- Promote a fully democratic Western Hemisphere, bound together by free trade

- Defend America's interests in the Persian Gulf and advance peace in the Middle East, based upon a secure Israel

- Check the contagious spread of weapons of mass destruction, and the means to deliver them

- Lead toward a world that trades in freedom

What Others Say

"George W. Bush's November 19 speech at the Reagan Library represents the strongest and clearest articulation of a policy of American global leadership by a major political figure since the collapse of the Soviet Empire. In his call for renewed American strength, confidence, and leadership, Bush stakes a claim to the legacy of Ronald Reagan."

Editorial, <u>Weekly Standard</u>, 11/22/99

"It may have been the best foreign policy speech given since the end of the Cold War, and will be a hard act for other Republican candidates to follow."

Editorial, <u>Washington Times</u>, 11/22/99

"Bush delivered his 35-minute speech with considerable aplomb, turning in a well-versed, well-drilled performance that...rose to a presidential level."

Johnny Apple, <u>The New York Times</u>, 11/20/99

"Very strong speech. I really do think maybe the strongest statement of the case for American global leadership since the end of the Cold War by a major political figure, a real Reaganite speech...That was a Reaganite speech, a Teddy Roosevelt speech. Pretty impressive performance, I thought."

Bill Kristol, ABC, "This Week," 11/21/99

"It was a well-written, well-delivered blueprint of international policy. It outlines some distinct differences in key areas with the Clinton administration."

Candy Crowley, CNN, "Inside Politics," 11/19/99

"George W. Bush outlined a broad-strokes foreign policy Friday whose bedrock principle is that free trade will promote free economies, which will in turn encourage democracies that promote freedom and protect human rights."

R.G. Ratcliffe, <u>Houston Chronicle</u>, 11/20/99

8

Agriculture:
The Heart of our Economy

Dallas Center, Iowa

September 1, 1999

We've got our work cut out for us. But hard work is what the American farmer knows best.

Agriculture is not just one industry among many. It is the heart of our economy. And it symbolizes some of the best and finest things about our nation: independence, hard work, risk-taking and sacrifice.

Farmers contribute to the wealth of America. But – with their commitment to faith, family and the land – they also contribute to the character of our country. I am honored to be the Governor of the second largest farm state. And I know when farmers hurt, we must help.

Today, the American farmer is facing a crisis – especially here in Iowa.

The problems are complicated, involving every kind of adversity, from bad weather to closed markets. But our response must be simple and direct.

First, we must get farmers the emergency assistance they need, in the form of direct payments. And, unlike last year's emergency aid, the help must come in time to meet the emergency.

The 1996 Farm Bill brought a lot of changes into the lives of farmers. In the long term, it promises much good – as farmers rely less on government control of supply and more on market demand. But this is today, not the long term, and we owe it to farmers to see them through the transition.

Second, we must reform the crop insurance system. At present only 60 percent of cultivated land is covered. Some crops and livestock aren't covered at all. And where coverage is available, the government's premium structure can make adequate coverage unaffordable. We need to change that. We need to cover more crops, to reform the government premium structure, and to encourage insurers to develop new methods of risk-management.

Third, we should create tax-deferred savings accounts that allow farmers to safeguard against downturns in the farm economy – permitting them to set aside a substantial percentage of their farm income for future needs. Down the road, these accounts will help in the tough years, like this one.

Next, some serious tax reform is in order – and it should begin with the death tax.

It has always amazed me that while trying to help farmers on one end through agriculture policies, the government punishes small farmers on the other end with this destructive tax. We make it impossible for families to carry on one generation after another, and then we wonder why America's small farms are vanishing.

Today death taxes on farms run as high as 55 percent, forcing many farmers to sell off land or equipment just to pay the government. It is bad policy, unwise and unfair. We must phase out death taxes on farms until this burden is eliminated.

In Texas, in my first term, we enacted one of the strongest property-rights laws in the nation. As president I would follow the same policies.

I know that farmers are on the front lines of advances in technology. This has led to new products and increased productivity. That is why I support value added processing. That is why I support ethanol to clean our air. And that is why we need to continue to support innovative uses for agricultural products, in the United States and abroad.

These are some of the things that must be done here at home, in changing the policies of our own government. More complex are the problems farmers face abroad, in exporting to foreign markets. Americans account for just 4 percent of the world's population. Clearly the farmer's greatest challenge – and opportunity – is to gain ground in the markets that feed the other 96 percent.

American farmers are without rival in their ability to produce and compete. Often the only thing that stands in your way are trade barriers built by foreign governments and tolerated by this Administration. They will not be tolerated in my administration.

The next president must reclaim the authority of the executive to negotiate new trade agreements. Every president from 1975 to 1994 has had that fast-track authority, until this president let it lapse. It is a powerful tool in prying open foreign markets, and never have we needed it more.

To foreign governments, the next president must also carry a simple and unequivocal message: We will no longer tolerate favoritism and unfair subsidies for your national industries. We want to compete, and compete on level ground.

I favor the so-called "single undertaking" approach to the next round of trade negotiations. That's diplomatic talk, and let me translate: Agriculture won't be left behind. I will use all the leverage at our disposal to open agriculture markets worldwide.

The next president must send an even more direct message to our European trading partners. Today, the European Union has a moratorium on the import of all but a handful of biotech crops. Yet the rules state clearly that health and safety regulations must be based on sound science. And study after study has shown no evidence of danger.

As president, I will have strong relations with the European Union. But I will not stand for unfair trade barriers. And that is what these objections to our biotech crops really are. They are trade barriers pure and simple – unfounded in science, unjustified in law, and unfair in practice.

Just as we oppose trade barriers abroad, however, we can not impose them on ourselves. Unilateral sanctions on agricultural exports only punish our own farmers, while helping our competitors. We are too good a people to use food as a weapon. In my administration, we will end this practice.

Finally, there is one other piece of unfinished business on the topic of trade. On the right terms, I believe we should bring China into the World Trade Organization as quickly as possible.

Earlier this year, when the Chinese tried to enter the WTO, their negotiators made some major concessions – agreeing to dramatically increase their purchases of bulk commodities like corn and wheat. The limits on corn imports, for example, would have risen from 250,000 metric tons to 7.2 million metric tons.

On top of that, China agreed to reduce tariffs on agricultural products, even below what most of our trading partners impose.

I have some serious concerns about China's record as a trading partner. But these were serious concessions, a good sign, and we should have taken them up on it. Bringing China within the rules of the world trading system is in China's own interest. More importantly it is in ours, because America's best export is freedom.

Crises come and go, but commitments do not. And these are my commitments to you. In our high-tech economy, with everything changing so quickly, I think there is a tendency to take the agriculture industry for granted. In a way, this is a tribute to farmers: America has long been the agricultural center of the world, and many just assume it will always be so.

But this will not always be true, unless we support American farmers as they have supported us. The American people have always been able to count on you. Now it is time that you, the farmers of America, were able to count on us.

Position Paper

Agriculture: The Heart of our Economy

"The American spirit shines bright in America's farmers: independent, hard working, entrepreneurial, with faith in their families, their labor and their land. In this downturn in the farm economy, we must provide farmers with the means to weather change. And we must fight hard to expand existing export markets - and pry open new ones - to fuel the future growth of the farm economy."

Governor George W. Bush

The U.S. Farm Sector

Agriculture is at the heart of the U.S. economy. The entire food and fiber sector – including agricultural production, transportation, and marketing – accounts for 13 percent of our nation's economic production. According to the American Farm Bureau, agriculture is the nation's largest employer, with more than 22 million people working in some phase of the industry, from growing food and fiber to selling it at the supermarket. Future prosperity of the U.S. farm sector depends in large part on expanding global markets for U.S. products:

- The U.S. leads the world in agricultural exports, with $53.7 billion in 1998, which generated an agricultural trade surplus of $16.7 billion.

- Nearly every state benefits from the income generated by agricultural exports, and nineteen states have exports of $1 billion or more.

As trade becomes an ever more important segment of the agriculture economy, Governor Bush is committed to opening markets and to finding new avenues for American products and American values.

Response to the Current Crisis

The 1996 Farm Bill reversed decades of supply control management, and unleashed U.S. farmers to plant in response to market demand, not government programs. After a period of growth, the farm economy has now weakened due to increased global production and slack demand, principally in Asia.

As the farm sector moves toward market-driven production, Governor Bush believes the government should help farmers adapt to a global marketplace by providing them with a strong safety net and the means to manage the cyclical downturns in the farm economy. That is why Governor Bush supports:

Additional emergency assistance to help farmers make the transition to a market-driven regime: The farm sector has been hit hard by the impact of large supplies and low prices. USDA economic projections for 1999 suggested continued low prices for several major farm commodities, such as cotton, corn, soybeans, and livestock, and further contraction of overseas markets. That is why Governor Bush supported additional emergency assistance, in the form of direct payments, consistent with the principles in the 1996 Farm Bill, to ensure that the move toward a market-oriented farm policy continues.

Reform of the crop insurance program: Under the current crop insurance program, 60 percent of cultivated land is covered by crop insurance. Governor Bush believes we must make it a priority to develop a crop insurance program that better reflects farmers' risk management needs, including policies that cover more commodities, including livestock, offer a wider variety of plans, more comprehensive coverage, and affordable premiums. At the same time, we should encourage the private sector to continue to develop new risk management tools, like the Crop Revenue Coverage and Revenue Assurance programs, which were developed in Iowa, and are now available in six states.

Tax Incentives

Incentives to encourage farmers and ranchers to establish tax-deferred accounts to help manage fluctuations in farm income: Governor Bush understands that "saving for a rainy day" has a literal meaning for farmers and ranchers. What they need are new tools to help them manage through cyclical downturns. That is why Governor Bush supports the creation of farm and ranch risk management accounts that would permit farmers to reserve a substantial percentage of their net farm income in a tax deferred account. These funds could be held in the account for several years and drawn upon in years of declining income to help farmers offset operation expenses and to purchase supplies for the next production cycle.

Eliminate the estate tax for family farms and ranches: Estate taxes can destroy family-owned farms, ranches, and small businesses, when the tax –

which can be as high as 55 percent – forces farmers and ranchers to sell land, buildings or equipment to pay the government. That is why Governor Bush's tax cut plan calls for eliminating the estate tax to allow farms, ranches and other small businesses to be passed, intact, from one generation to the next.

New Technologies

Farmers are on the front lines of the new "knowledge-based" economy. Advances in technology are leading to new products, increased productivity, and more environmentally friendly farming. For the U.S. agricultural economy to remain competitive, we must support projects that will generate new exportable goods. That is why Governor Bush supports:

- Agriculture research and education activities that help develop technologically advanced farm products for market here in the United States and for export to our world partners; and

- Permanent extension of the research and development tax credit.

Ethanol and Alternative Uses of Agricultural Products

Governor Bush is committed to the continuing search for innovative uses for agricultural products, especially environmentally beneficial uses. That is why he supports ethanol. Ethanol helps our farmers and makes air cleaner.

Governor Bush believes we need to accelerate our search for innovative uses for farm products. For example, research into biomass technology could develop efficient fuels and other chemicals from virtually any plant or plant product. This type of research could become even more important for fuels like ethanol, given emerging evidence regarding the potential environmental damage from the fuel additive MTBE (methyl tertiary butyl ether). As President, he would encourage the development of new technologies for cost-effectively producing ethanol, bio-diesel fuel and other bio-fuels and products.

Regulation

Governor Bush recognizes that burdensome regulations have a real cost impact to the farm economy. That is why Governor Bush believes that regulations should be based on sound science and common sense, and solutions should involve local input, wherever possible.

Private Property Rights

Governor Bush understands that private property is fundamental to our way of life and the backbone of our economy. In his first term as Governor of Texas, he signed one of the strongest private property rights laws in the nation. As President, Governor Bush would require that the federal government carefully evaluate the impact of regulatory initiatives on private property rights. In the event that the government, acting on behalf of all citizens, asks private landowners to refrain from utilizing land, Governor Bush believes that the landowners should receive just compensation for their loss.

Livestock Price Reporting

Governor Bush believes that in order to ensure a healthy agricultural economy we must guard against potential anti-competitive practices. He recognizes that increased concentration is a growing concern among farmers and ranchers. He believes that ensuring transparent and accurate price reporting is important to ensure a competitive market. That is why Governor Bush supports the livestock industry's efforts to work together to formulate a policy that guarantees accurate, fair, and open price reporting. As President, his administration will diligently work to maintain competitive markets and ensure that existing anti-trust laws are enforced.

Kyoto Protocol

Governor Bush does not support the Kyoto Protocol to the UN Framework on Climate Change. Economists predict that reducing emissions to the level called for in the treaty will require major new taxes, or increases in key farm inputs, such as fuel, fertilizer and farm chemicals. Furthermore, for the countries included in the agreement, the negative economic impact may outweigh the minor environmental benefits. At the same time, the Kyoto Protocol exempts major competitors such as China and Mexico from these costly regulations, which could result in U.S. farmers and ranchers being disadvantaged in the competitive world of international trade. That is why Governor Bush believes that before any agreement on climate change is signed, an honest and thorough assessment must be completed to estimate the impact on the American economy as a whole – and on the farm sector in particular.

Food Quality Protection Act

Governor Bush supports the 1996 Food Quality Protection Act (FQPA). He recognizes, however, that the FQPA presents many challenges, and believes that several key concerns need to be addressed in its implementation:

- The Environmental Protection Agency and other agencies should proceed to implement the new law in a manner that does not disrupt farmers' access to safe crop protection products.

- New requirements under the FQPA should not be implemented in a manner that restricts the use of valuable crop protection tools unless viable alternatives are available.

International Trade

Governor Bush is committed to free trade. He will work to tear down barriers everywhere and will use every available tool to combat unfair trade practices. Governor Bush is confident that America's best is the best in the world. To lead the world on trade and open markets for U.S. farmers, Governor Bush believes we must:

Pass presidential trade negotiating authority so we can negotiate market-opening agreements: Every President since Ford has had this authority, which the Clinton-Gore Administration let expire in 1994, and have been unable to renew this important tool for trade negotiations. This has not only hobbled this Administration's ability to pry open foreign markets, but undermined America's fundamental ability to lead global market-opening efforts. As President, Governor Bush will work with Congress to renew presidential trade negotiating authority.

Open global agricultural markets: The recent failure to initiate a new trade round in Seattle underscores the administration's lack of leadership on trade. As President, Governor Bush will work to launch a new trade round that will level the agricultural playing field once and for all by completely eliminating agricultural export subsidies and tariffs worldwide.

Eliminating Barriers to Safe Food: In 1999, 50 percent of the soybeans, 40 percent of the cotton, and about one-third of the corn produced in the U.S. was genetically modified. The European Union, however, imposed a moratorium on the import of new biotech crops. Additionally, despite a ruling of the World

Trade Organization, the european community continues to ban the import of U.S. beef treated with growth hormones. World Trade Organization rules clearly state that health and safety regulations must be based on sound science. As President, Governor Bush will fight to ensure that U.S. products are allowed entry into the European Union and require them to use accepted scientific principles in enacting their regulations.

Exempt food from unilateral trade sanctions and embargoes: Unilateral trade sanctions are rarely effective in achieving their foreign policy goals, and often force U.S. businesses and farmers to lose market share to foreign competitors. That is why Governor Bush believes that, if sanctions are used, they should be directed at the offending government, not innocent populations, and food and medicine exports should be exempt from any new unilateral sanctions.

China-WTO Membership: Governor Bush believes that on the right terms, admitting China to the World Trade Organization is in America's interest. It will provide U.S. farmers, ranchers, and businesses access to a growing market, and will help introduce American values along with American products.

THE TEXAS RECORD

As the Governor of the second-largest agriculture producing state, Governor Bush has led Texas in implementing innovative policies to support the continued growth of the farm sector. Specifically, Governor Bush:

- Signed into law the "Agriculture and Rural Development Act," which created the state's first comprehensive agriculture policy.

- Appropriated $25 million in emergency spending and $50 million in cost sharing assistance to aid with boll weevil eradication, providing over 23,000 producers with support during an especially difficult crop season.

- Signed into law "The Young Farmer Loan Guarantee Program," that expanded the Texas Agriculture Financing Authority to provide $225 million in loan guarantees to assist in rural development and value-added agriculture production.

- In his first term, Governor Bush led the successful fight for passage of one of the strongest laws on private property rights in the nation.

175

What Others Say

"George W. Bush…is committed to opening international markets to our farm products, enhancing value-added agriculture and restoring profitability for farmers."

Former Iowa Governor Terry Branstad

"Governor Bush understands the importance of agriculture. He is committed to ethanol. He grew up in Texas cattle country where people are self-sufficient, independent and committed to the values of home, family and personal responsibility. These are the same values that make South Dakota great, and George W. Bush understands that."

U.S. Representative John Thune (R-SD-At-Large)

"American agriculture is in the midst of tough times. I am honored Governor Bush has chosen to make FARRM Accounts the number one item in his proposal to aid America's farmers and ranchers. As governor of the second-largest agriculture-producing state, Bush knows the importance of implementing innovative policies to help alleviate some of the financial burdens faced by those who make a living through agriculture."

U.S. Representative Kenny Hulshof (R-MO-9)

"I'm especially drawn to the track record Governor Bush has established on issues important to Iowans such as education, tax relief, and, with many Iowa farmers facing financial crisis, and his understanding of the rural economy."

Brent Siegrist, Iowa House Speaker

What Others Say

"I've been very impressed with Governor Bush's program for agriculture... His emphasis on expanding markets and reduced regulation is the kind of leadership North Dakota farmers are looking for."

**Susan Larson of Gilby, North Dakota,
GOP Vice-Chair District 19**

"The people in agriculture in Texas strongly support Governor George W. Bush because he has been such a strong supporter of agriculture," said Commissioner Combs. "He understands the plight and the problems of the men and women of agriculture, and it's my firm belief that when elected President, he will be an outstanding advocate for agriculture, which is this nation's bedrock."

Texas Agriculture Commissioner Susan Combs, 12/10/99

"Governor Bush understands the issues facing families across the Midwest. His successful record as Texas Governor, his plan for better schools and lower taxes, and his commitment to America's farmers will make George W. Bush a great President."

Bob Kjellander, Illinois Republican National Committeeman

"We are impressed with your record as Governor of Texas...As a successful Governor of an economically diverse state you understand the challenges facing agriculture and South Dakota...We strongly urge you to seek the Presidency of the United States, and to that effort we commit to you our support."

**South Dakota State Senate Majority Leader Mike Rounds
and State House Majority Leader Steve Cutler in a
letter to Governor Bush.**

9

High Tech:
Taking the Side of Innovation

Phoenix, Arizona

October 18, 1999

This summer in Silicon Valley, I faulted the Clinton administration for opposing limits on Y2K litigation, for imposing barriers on encryption technology, and for opposing a permanent tax credit for research and development. Since then, the administration has reversed itself on Y2K litigation, reversed itself on encryption exports, and reversed itself on tax credits for R&D. Now that's what I call responsive government! If I had only known they were going to grant me three wishes, I might have asked for something else.

With this administration, wisdom comes so rarely, we should not complain when it comes late. There is a difference between last-minute concessions and enthusiastic support – between reaction and initiative. And your industry these past seven years has spent enough time worrying about what might come next from Washington. If I am president, I will always take the side of innovation over litigation, and private initiative over federal regulation.

I'm here today to talk about policy, but also to share what's in my heart.

I'm running for president because our country must be prosperous. But prosperity must have a purpose. The purpose of prosperity is to make sure the American dream touches every willing heart. The purpose of prosperity is to leave no one out... to leave no one behind.

Prosperity is not a given, and governments do not create it. Wealth is created by Americans – by creativity and enterprise and risk-taking. These are the hallmarks of the high tech industry, where the great engine of wealth has become the human mind – creating value out of genius.

The role of government is to create an environment where businesses and entrepreneurs and families can dream and flourish.

We'll be prosperous if we reduce taxes. I'll have a plan that reduces marginal rates to create jobs, but a plan that also helps struggling families on the outskirts of poverty.

We'll be prosperous if we reduce the regulations that strangle enterprise. And I will do what I did in Texas: fight for meaningful, real tort reform.

We'll be prosperous if we embrace free trade. I'll work to end tariffs and break down barriers everywhere, entirely, so the whole world trades in freedom. The fearful build walls. The confident demolish them. I am confident in American workers and farmers and producers. And I am confident that America's best is the best in the world.

Our current technology export system just doesn't work. The administration seemed to concede this last month when, after years of talk and delay, it reversed itself on the sale and export of encryption technologies. Now the industry will have to wait and see how this new policy actually takes shape – whether it truly frees our technology exports, or whether it simply adds a few more layers of bureaucracy.

My policy as president would be to safeguard genuine military technology, while letting Americans sell what is already widely available elsewhere.

I support congressional efforts to reauthorize the Export Administration Act. The final bill must include a change in the criteria governing high-tech exports. Export controls that do not serve any clear national-security purpose will be eliminated. The new set of controls will no longer be based on technical specifications. Instead, we will guide our decisions by the availability of technologies in mass markets and foreign markets.

Our best companies have felt frustrated that they cannot sell some of their products abroad – even when equivalent technology is sold by foreign competitors. Those controls aren't serving the cause of America's security – they are a disservice to America's economic strength

I will also form an advisory board answering directly to the president on all matters relating to high tech exports. Too often, the federal government's export policies are arbitrary and irrational – overtaken by the very technology they attempt to regulate. Yesterday's supercomputer is today's laptop. Yet current rules don't take this into account. And there has been too little opportunity for America's high tech exporters to make their case about what should be restricted and what should not. This advisory board – the President's Technology Export Council – will give you that opportunity. It will work quickly, with a simple mandate: Wherever there is no security interest at stake, exports will be permitted. Wherever security is truly at stake, exports will be barred, with serious penalties for violations. And we will work to renew the cooperation of our allies in this effort.

There need not be any conflict between America's security interests abroad and our economic interests. We just need to be smart enough and flexible enough to distinguish between the technologies that guide enemy missiles and the technologies that animate children's games.

There is an irony here. While this administration has restricted high-tech exports – fearing these products might fall into the wrong hands – it has done little to develop our own military technologies here at home. They have actually cut our research and development investment by almost a billion dollars a year.

Last month in South Carolina I outlined my plans for the transformation of our military. America now has a tremendous opportunity – given few nations in history – to extend the current peace into the far realm of the future. This opportunity is created by a revolution in the technology of war. Power is increasingly defined, not by mass or size, but by mobility and swiftness. Influence is measured in information, safety is gained in stealth, and force is projected on the long arc of precision-guided weapons.

This revolution perfectly matches the strengths of our country – the skill of our people and the superiority of our technology. The best way to keep the peace is to redefine war on our terms.

Central to that goal is a greater emphasis on research and development. Step one is to commit an additional $20 billion dollars to defense R&D between the time I take office and 2006. Step two is to encourage long-term private investment in research and development by making the R&D tax credit permanent.

As it is, high-tech companies are often hesitant to undertake long-term research projects because they cannot count on that tax credit. It might be renewed, it might not. Yet it is exactly this kind of sustained, long-term R&D our country needs to gain the next generation of critical technologies – both military and civilian. If we as a nation wish to continue to enjoy strong economic growth, continued military superiority, and unrivaled technological leadership, then we must reverse this decline in R&D and invest in our future.

So America will be prosperous if we do the right things. But prosperity alone is simple materialism. Prosperity must have a greater purpose. The success of America has never been proven by cities of gold, but by citizens of character. Men and women who work hard, dream big, love their family, serve their neighbor. Values that turn a piece of earth into a neighborhood, a community, a chosen nation.

That dream is so vivid – but too many are saying: The dream is not for me. Kids who turn schoolyards into battlefields. Children who corrupt their wills and souls with drugs, who limit their ambitions by having children themselves. Failed schools are creating two societies: one that reads and one that can't; one that dreams and one that doesn't.

These are burdens on the conscience of a successful nation. The next president must close this gap of hope. It is the great challenge to America's good heart.

I want to be a president who sets a tone, a direction, an agenda. I will be an activist president, who sets goals worthy of a great nation. I won't use my office as a mirror to reflect public opinion. And I'll be guided by conservative principles. Government should do a few things, and do them well. Government should not try to be all things to all people.

My first goal is to usher in the responsibility era. An era that stands in stark contrast to the last few decades, when the culture has clearly said: If it feels good, do it. If you've got a problem, blame someone else. Each of us must understand we are responsible for the choices we make in life.

We're responsible for the children we bring into the world. We're responsible to love our neighbor as we want to be loved ourselves

The prosperous need to be generous. It is a responsibility that comes with success, as many of you realize. The amazing prosperity of the new economy must be applied to a higher purpose. Economic entrepreneurs need to become social entrepreneurs, using their creativity to help reform schools and confront poverty.

And we must pass this message of responsibility to our children – teach them there are right choices in life and wrong choices in life. Drugs will destroy you. Alcohol will ruin your life. And having a child out of wedlock is a sure fire way to fall behind. We'll love the babies. But the message must be clear: It is not the definition of a man to father a child out of wedlock and say, "They're not my problem, they're yours."

Some people think it's inappropriate to draw a moral line. Not me. For our children to have the lives we want for them, they must learn to say yes to responsibility, yes to family, yes to honesty and work. I have seen our culture change once in my lifetime, so I know it can change again.

Government can help. We can write laws to give schools and principals more authority to discipline children and protect the peace of classrooms. We must encourage states to reform their juvenile justice laws. We must say to our children, "We love you, but discipline and love go hand in hand, and there will be bad consequences for bad behavior."

But changing our culture requires more than laws. Cultures change one heart, one soul, one conscience at a time. Government can spend money, but it can't put hope in our hearts or a sense of purpose in our lives. This is done by churches and synagogues and mosques and charities that warm the cold of life. A quiet river of goodness and kindness that cuts through stone.

So my second goal – one of the biggest jobs for the next president – is to rally these armies of compassion that exist in every community. To nurture. To mentor. To comfort. To perform their commonplace miracles of renewal.

As president, I will lift the regulations that hamper them. I will involve them in after-school programs, maternity group homes, drug treatment, prison ministries. I will lay out specific incentives to encourage an outpouring of giving in America. Supporting these men and women – the soldiers in the army of compassion – is the next, bold step of welfare reform. Because changing hearts will change our entire society.

And my third goal: We should make a solemn commitment in this country: That every child will be educated. That no child will be left behind.

This is urgent in our new economy. Our nation must have a workforce prepared to seize new opportunity. In the short-term, America should be able to benefit from the immigration of skilled workers. The limit on H-1B visas should be raised.

But the long-term solution is better schools with higher standards. I've seen what works in Texas. Measure progress. Insist on results. Blow the whistle on failure. Emphasize early reading, early intervention, math and science instruction. End social promotion. Above all, don't give up on anyone.

I believe that children, not systems, are sacred. I believe that the educational oligopoly has little incentive to reform itself. That's why I believe in charter schools and choice to challenge the status quo.

Everyone must have a first rate education, because there are no second rate children, no second rate dreams.

You've heard me talk about compassionate conservatism. These goals are what I mean.

It is conservative to cut taxes. It is compassionate to let people keep more of their own money to save and give and build.

It is conservative to reform welfare by insisting on work. It is compassionate to take the side of charities and churches that confront the suffering which remains.

It is conservative to confront illegitimacy. It is compassionate to offer practical help to women and children in crisis.

It is conservative to insist on education standards, basics and local control. It is compassionate to make sure that not one single child gets left behind.

I am proud to be a compassionate conservative. I welcome the label. And on this ground I'll take my stand.

It is the ground I've stood as governor of Texas, a job I really love. I know it isn't the same as being president. But if Texas were a country, it would be the 11th largest economy in the world. And I've had some successes. We passed the two biggest tax cuts in Texas history. We reformed our welfare and tort laws. We improved test scores for all the children in our schools, especially African-American and Hispanic kids.

I've learned to lead. I know how to set a clear agenda and get results.

I've learned you can not lead by dividing people. I'm a uniter not a divider. And I know my most important responsibility is when I put my hand on the Bible, I will not only swear to uphold the laws of our country. I will swear to uphold the dignity of the office of President of the United States of America.

This country is hungry for a new style of campaign. Positive. Hopeful. Inclusive. A campaign that attracts new faces and new voices.

A campaign that unites all Americans toward a better tomorrow.

We will prove that someone who is conservative and compassionate can win without sacrificing principle. We will show that politics, after a time of tarnished ideals, can be higher and better. We will give our country a fresh start after a season of cynicism.

We have a long way to go, but we are starting. And I hope you'll join me.

Position Paper
High Technology

"Governments don't create wealth. Wealth is created by Americans – by creativity and enterprise and risk-taking. The great engine of wealth has become the human mind – creating value out of genius. The role of government is to create an environment where business-es and entrepreneurs and families can flourish."

Governor George W. Bush

Technology and the Economy

Americans have always been leaders in technology, and technology has always played an integral part in our nation's history. But in an unprecedented way, technology is taking center stage in the American economy:

- The high technology elements of our economy accounted for over a third of real economic growth in the United States between 1995 and 1998.

- In 1999, Internet-related companies generated more than $500 billion in revenue in the United States and were responsible for 2.3 million jobs. The Internet Economy is projected to be worth $1 trillion by 2001.

Governor Bush is committed to ensuring that the engine of technological growth – young minds and compassionate character – is supported by an educational system that teaches every child to learn to read and leaves no child behind.

Accordingly, as President, he will set three main priorities in the high technology sector:

Goal #1: Lift barriers to innovation and fight efforts in the United States and overseas to impose new obstacles

The world is changing and so must the attitude of government.

To ensure the competitiveness of American's high tech sector, Governor Bush will:

<u>Fight to achieve meaningful, real tort reform</u>: Governor Bush understands that many of the most innovative technology companies are startups and small businesses that are particularly vulnerable to frivolous and junk lawsuits. Thus, as President, he will fight to achieve what he did in Texas: meaningful, real tort reform. He is committed to ending the stream of frivolous and junk lawsuits that clog our courts, threaten our economy and delay justice for the deserving.

<u>Pursue an international agenda that supports America's high technology companies</u>: Governor Bush understands that to be prosperous we must embrace free trade. As President, he will fight to tear down the international barriers to innovation that have already been raised, and work to ensure that new ones are not erected. Among other things, he will work to:

- Make the Internet a duty and tariff-free zone worldwide.

- Tear down non-tariff barriers to trade in information technology.

- Step up efforts to combat piracy of American ideas and intellectual property.

- Promote the development of internationally compatible standards for e-commerce.

<u>Develop a tough-minded, common sense export control system that safeguards military technology, while allowing U.S. companies to sell technology that is readily available in the commercial market</u>: The current system of export controls is broken. Too often it penalizes our high tech companies by controlling technology that is widely available from other countries, while failing to prevent unique technology from falling into dangerous hands. Moreover, controls often lag behind technological developments. And because the international regime for coordinating export controls was disbanded under the Clinton-Gore Administration, the United States now frequently finds itself trying to single-handedly prevent diversion of sensitive technology.

Governor Bush is committed to developing a tough-minded, common sense export policy – a policy that places a priority on safeguarding our national security, while recognizing that the competitiveness of our high technology sector is itself a critical component of that security. Such a policy must consist of several key elements:

- First and foremost, we must strengthen America's intelligence and counterintelligence capabilities to staunch the theft of sensitive military technology at home, and identify threats abroad before they arise.

- Second, we must allow American companies to sell products in the international marketplace when those products are readily available from their foreign competitors. That means easing export controls on computers and encryption products that can already be purchased on the open market. At the same time, as the use of encryption programs increases, American law enforcement must always have the resources to stay ahead of the criminal use of that technology.

- Third, as the Cox Report recommends, the United States must lead its allies in establishing new, binding rules to prevent the export of sensitive military technology. The United States must no longer be alone in keeping dangerous technologies and products away from those who do not wish us well.

Goal #2: Help our nation develop and maintain a workforce prepared to seize the opportunities of the high technology economy

The new "knowledge-based" economy depends upon a skilled and educated workforce.

To ensure that America's high tech companies have access to the best employees, Governor Bush will:

<u>Maintain the competitiveness of our high technology companies by allowing them to recruit more workers with special skills through an increase in the current limit on "H-1B" visas</u>: Temporary highly-skilled workers are admitted under H-1B visas, which are limited to 115,000 per year. In FY2000, this number is expected to be reached by the middle of the year, creating a backlog in demand that could hurt high tech industries that are currently facing a shortage of computer engineers, software programmers and technicians.

<u>Reform the schools that do not work and will not change by eliminating</u> <u>oligopolies, raising standards, measuring progress, and blowing the whis-</u> <u>tle on failure</u>: The long-term solution to a shortage of prepared workers is not immigration. It is education. Governor Bush believes in the power of high standards and high hopes. As President, George W. Bush will give more flexibility and authority to states – but encourage local authorities to measure results for every child. If schools fail, we must be bold enough to challenge the status quo.

Goal #3: Establish a stable environment that encourages research and innovation in the private sector and the military

American needs sustained, long-term investment in R&D to develop the next generation of critical technology, both civilian and military.

As President, Governor Bush will:

<u>Support a permanent tax credit for research and development</u>: The Research and Experimentation Tax Credit encourages long-term invest- ment in research by high technology companies and thereby strengthens America's technological leadership. Since its inception in 1981, the bene- fits of the credit were dampened by the temporary, on-again, off-again nature of this credit which confused and disrupted corporate planning. This year, Congress took a step in the right direction by passing a five-year extension of the credit. As President, George W. Bush will lead the Congress to make the credit a permanent part of our tax code.

<u>Strengthen research and development in the military</u>: A substantially greater emphasis on research and development will be required to ensure that our military is fully prepared to meet future challenges and to realize the full promise of new technology. As President, Governor Bush will increase the defense R&D budget by $20 billion from FY 2002-FY2006 and will direct the Secretary of Defense to earmark at least 20 per cent of the total procurement budget for acquisitions programs that propel America generations ahead in military technology.

THE TEXAS RECORD

During Governor Bush's term in office, Texas has led the nation in high- tech job growth. Between 1995 and 1997, over 62,200 high-tech jobs were created, making Texas second in the nation for high-tech employment. More than 90 percent of Texas public schools now have Internet access, and all 57 community colleges are receiving state technology grants.

In 1996, Governor Bush created the Science and Technology Council to devise a strategic plan to ensure Texas remains at the forefront in high-tech job growth. As a result, Governor Bush and the Texas Legislature acted on the Council's recommendations and:

- Provided a research and development tax credit to help Texas attract high-skilled, high-paying jobs.

- Increased funding from $2 million to $21 million for the high school Advanced Placement program to increase the number of high school graduates with high level math and science skills. The increased funding will provide more classes per high school, reduce the cost of the test for low income students, and provide teacher training.

- Developed a statewide technology curriculum for community colleges to better prepare students for the demands of high technology employment.

Under Governor Bush's leadership, Texas:

- Cut the state Internet access and data processing tax.

- Created an E-Government Task Force to evaluate opportunities to interact with citizens, universities and other states online.

- Enacted legislation to provide legal protections for companies that make good faith efforts to address Y2K-related problems.

- Passed comprehensive tort reform measures that will discourage frivolous and junk lawsuits by limiting punitive damage awards, making joint and several liability more fair, and increasing sanctions for those filing frivolous lawsuits. As a result, Texans have enjoyed $2.9 billion in insurance rate reductions.

- Created the second largest government-operated telecommunications network in the nation, which has achieved over $10 million in annual savings while providing discounted services to schools, colleges and universities, libraries, hospitals, and telemedicine entities.

What Others Say

"Brian Halla, chief executive of National Semiconductor, said: 'People talk about the administration coming out here once every two months in the last few years, but I can tell you that Governor Bush can walk the walk and talk the talk.'… Bob Herbold, chief operating officer of Microsoft, who travelled from Washington state to the Bush breakfast, said: [Bush] has strong support from the high-tech community…"

Richard Wolffe, "Bush Woos Silicon Valley,"
Financial Times, 7/2/99

"New Economy leaders should support Texas Gov. George W. Bush for president because he has shown through his record in Texas that he knows what it takes to help this digital economy thrive. He shares the economic and philosophical principles that promote the entrepreneurial spirit that has brought us the Information Age: excellence in education, less litigation, limited government, less regulation, less taxation, and strong trade."

E. Floyd Kvamme, Partner at venture capital firm
Kleiner Perkins Caufield & Byers

"[T]he Bush plan is attractive to the aspiring and inventive [by making] the Research and Development tax credit a permanent part of tax law."

Fernando Oaxaca, _The Oaxaca Journal_, 12/1/99

What Others Say

"'I think the governor understands the high-tech industry is driving our growth. He gets the message. And, by the way, he expects the industry to play a key role in society as well – to give back,' said John Chambers, CEO of Cisco Systems."

Mary Anne Ostrom, <u>San Jose Mercury News</u>, 7/2/99

"[George W. Bush] was obviously out here yesterday...in Silicon Valley in Palo Alto. A huge turnout...Gordon Moore, the co-founder of Intel, Ray Lane, the president of Oracle, John Chambers, CEO of Cisco Systems, all clapping... or jumped onto the Bush bandwagon...[T]here were several issues he outlined including increasing the number of visas for skilled workers, very important to Silicon Valley...easing restrictions on exporting computer systems overseas... There were several other issues like that which all came forward and really for the first time I think Silicon Valley could see that they have a real choice..."

Tony Perkins, Editor-in-Chief, Red Herring
CNNFN,"Digital Jam," 7/2/99

"In a rousing speech to Silicon Valley executives, George W. Bush yesterday attacked President Clinton's handling of Y2K legislation and promised lower taxes and easier immigration rules for the high-tech industry. The enthusiastic response by the 500 high-tech executives demonstrated that Democrat front-runner Al Gore's grip on the prosperous region is less than firm, despite years of careful political cultivation…"

Carla Marinucci and Robert B. Gunnison,
"Bush Hits Right Notes in Silicon Valley,"
<u>The San Francisco Chronicle</u>, 7/2/99

10

Positions Taken on the Issues

Education:

- Outlined a plan to give states, local districts and parents more authority to set priorities and chart the path to greater student achievement
- Supports making federal funds to states and local districts more flexible in return for greater accountability and improved student achievement
- Called for the creation of "charter states" – states that would receive maximum flexibility with federal funds in return for meeting high performance measures in increasing student achievement
- Supports implementation of state accountability systems in which students are tested every year in grades 3-8 in reading and math. States will be free to choose their own tests, and the federal government will equally share the cost
- Supports paying for states to participate in an annual National Assessment in Education Progress sample exam in reading and math to gauge progress
- Supports establishing a $500 million incentive fund to reward states for improving student performance
- Supports establishing a reward fund to reward schools that show the greatest improvements in student achievement
- Supports empowering parents with information by requiring states to publish school-by-school report cards with annual test results
- Supports increasing choices for parents in the education of their children by allowing federal funds to be used for public and private school choice and innovative education programs

- Supports expanding education savings accounts for parents to increase their annual contributions from $500 per student to $5,000 and withdraw funds tax free to pay for education expenses from Kindergarten to college

- Supports establishing a Charter School Homestead Fund to provide $3 billion of loan guarantees to help establish or improve 2,000 charter schools nationwide in two years

- Supports giving parents of Title I students trapped in persistently failing schools federal education dollars in a portable account to use in a school or program of their choice

- Called for the reform of Head Start to ensure children are ready for school by teaching pre-reading and numeracy skills that will put them on the path to literacy

- Supports moving Head Start from the Department of Education to emphasize a renewed focus on education preparedness

- Supports increased and focused research in education to determine what works in educating children

- Establish "Project Sentry" – a federal-state partnership to prosecute juveniles who bring guns to school or use them illegally and the adults who provide guns

- Expect states and districts to establish a "zero tolerance" policy on disruption, empowering teachers to remove violent or persistently disruptive students from the classroom

- Enact a "Teacher Protection Act" to shield teachers, principals, and school board members from meritless lawsuits arising from their efforts to maintain discipline

- Require states and districts to provide all students in persistently dangerous schools with the option of transferring to a safe school

- Triple character education funding and incorporate character-building lessons into federal youth programs

- Hold states and districts receiving federal School Safety funds accountable for measuring and demonstrating improved safety

- Call for a uniform reporting system on school safety and publish the results widely

- Establish the "American Youth Character Awards" to honor acts of character in America's young people
- Lift barriers to information being shared between schools and law enforcement agencies

Taxes:

Outlined a bold plan which includes:

- Doubles the child credit to $1,000
- Replaces the current five rate structure of 15, 28, 31, 36, and 39.6 percent with four, lower rates: 10, 15, 25, and 33 percent
- Expands the charitable deduction to non-itemizers
- Increases the annual contribution limit on Educational Savings Accounts from $500 to $5,000, and expanding them beyond college, down to Kindergarten
- Eliminates the death tax
- Restores the Reagan 10 percent deduction for two-income married couples, greatly reducing the marriage penalty
- Eliminates the Social Security earnings test

- Supports an extension of the moratorium on Internet sales taxation at least through 2004
- Opposes taxes on access to the Internet
- Would veto any increase in personal or corporate income tax rates

Social Security:

- Pledged to fulfill the solemn commitment of Social Security; no reduction in benefits for retirees or near retirees
- Called for dedicating all Social Security money to Social Security (lock box)
- Opposes any tax increase for Social Security
- Supports making personal retirement accounts part of Social Security reform
- Opposes government investment in private stocks or bonds

Medicare/Health Care:

- Wants to strengthen Medicare by providing more choice and more private sector alternatives for the elderly

- Supports offering a prescription drug benefit to Medicare recipients through more options and greater choice of plans; also supports giving financial assistance to poor seniors to help pay for the plans

- Supports medical savings accounts as a health insurance option for all Americans

- Supports giving patients in federally governed health care plans protections similar to those already enacted in Texas; opposes legislation that would supersede reforms already enacted by states

Highlights of the Texas reforms include:

- Allow patients to appeal denials of care to an independent review panel and in some cases take the HMO to court

- Require coverage and payment of emergency services

- Allow patients to choose their own doctor, outside their plan, as long as they are willing to pay any additional cost

- Require report cards on the performance of HMOs

- Prohibit "gag clauses," which discourage doctors from communicating with patients regarding treatment options

- Require HMOs to give women direct access to their obstetrician-gynecologists

Defense:

- Supports rebuilding America's military strength to keep the peace

- Would increase by $1 billion the recently passed military pay raise to encourage the best and brightest to enlist – and reenlist – in the armed forces

- Would renovate substandard military housing and improve military training

- Would maintain longstanding U.S. commitments, but order an immediate review of overseas deployments in dozens of countries, with the aim of replacing uncertain missions with well-defined objectives

- Would deter terrorist attacks by ensuring that every group or nation understands that if they sponsor such attacks, the U.S. response will be devastating

- Supports accelerated research for and deployment of both theater missile defenses and national missile defense, as soon as possible

- Prepared to cancel ABM treaty with Russia if unable to convince Russia to amend the treaty to allow deployment of missile defense systems within a short period of time

- Would strengthen our intelligence community's ability to detect terrorist threats, and develop long-range strike capabilities to eliminate such threats before they arise

- Would promote cooperation with our allies, who should share the burden of defense

- Would order a comprehensive military review to develop a new architecture for American defense designed to meet the challenges of the next century

- Would seize the opportunity to skip a generation of weapons, not merely improving existing systems, but replacing them with a new generation of technology

- Would earmark at least 20 percent of the procurement budget for acquisition programs that propel America generations ahead in military technology

- Would increase defense R&D spending by at least $20 billion from FY2002 to FY2006

- Supports a continued moratorium on nuclear testing, and opposed ratification of the Comprehensive Test Ban Treaty

Foreign Policy:

- Would refocus America's policy in Asia on friends and allies

- Would redefine relationship between China and U.S. as one of "competitors," not strategic partners

- Supports "one-China" policy

- Supports the Taiwan Relations Act
- Supports the Taiwan Security Enhancement Act
- Opposes any further IMF loans to Russia
- Would work with Russia to achieve verifiable strategic arms reduction and prevent the spread of nuclear weapons
- Would press Moscow for an accurate inventory of all Russian nuclear material
- Would substantially increase funding for the Nunn-Lugar program in order to dismantle as many of Russia's nuclear weapons as possible, as quickly as possible
- Would redirect American assistance, investment and loans to the Russian people, not to the bank accounts of corrupt officials
- Supports reaching out to a new generation of Russians through educational exchanges and programs to support the rule of law and a civil society
- Would support the nations of the Baltics, the Caucasus and Central Asia, along with Ukraine, by promoting regional peace and economic development, and opening links to the wider world
- Would withhold international financial assistance from Russia because of the Russian government's attacks against civilians in Chechnya
- Would work with India to increase trade and investment and ensure that India is a force for stability and security in Asia
- Would work to strengthen NATO and America's other alliances through greater consultation and sustained American leadership
- Supports moving the U.S. embassy in Israel from Tel Aviv to Jerusalem and he would set the process of moving the Embassy in motion immediately upon taking office
- Would work to reestablish weapons inspections in Iraq
- Supports keeping the current sanctions on Cuba until there are free elections, free speech and freedom for political prisoners
- Supports helping America's friend and longstanding ally Australia with logistical support in East Timor

- Supported U.S. intervention in Kosovo because it was in our strategic interests

- Said option of ground troops should not have been taken off the table in Kosovo intervention

- Would never place U.S. troops under U.N. command

- Supports a U.N. role in weapons inspections, peacekeeping and humanitarian efforts

- Supports payment of dues to the United Nations only if its bureaucracy is reformed and America's disproportionate share of its costs is reduced

- Would press for reform at international financial institutions such as the IMF and the World Bank, including greater transparency and accountability at these institutions themselves

Proposals to Promote Faith-Based and Community Organizations:

- Lift federal regulations that hamper faith-based institutions from involvement in the delivery of services to the needy

- Expand the federal charitable deduction to taxpayers who do not itemize

- Permit a credit against state taxes for contributions to charities addressing poverty

- Permit individuals over 59 to contribute IRA funds to charities, without having to pay income tax on the amount withdrawn

- Raise the cap on corporate charitable deductions from 10% to 15% of a company's taxable income

- Provide civil liability protection for corporate in-kind donations of equipment or facilities to charities

- Expand "Charitable Choice" to all federal social service programs, allowing religious organizations to be eligible for funding on the same basis as any other provider, without impairing their religious character

- Establish an "Office of Faith-Based Action" in the Executive Office of the President

- Provide federal matching funds for the establishment of state offices of faith-based action

- Promote alternative licensing regimes that recognize religious training as an alternative form of qualification for delivery of non-medical social services

- Launch a new program, offering competitive grants to faith-based and community groups, to address the needs of children of prisoners

- Open certain federal after-school programs to faith-based and community groups

- Fund certificates to help lower-income parents pay for after-school activities

- Establish a "Compassion Capital Fund" – a public/private partnership to identify and invest in charitable "best practices"

- Make performance-based drug treatment grants available to the states and ensure that non-medical, faith-based providers are eligible for funds on the same basis as other groups

- Provide funding for pilot, faith-based prison pre-release programs

- Establish pilot "Second Chance" maternity homes, through a block grant to the states for certificates to individuals or competitive grants to providers

High Tech:

- Supports making the R&D Tax Credit permanent

- Supports increasing defense R&D spending by at least $20 billion from FY 2002-2006

- Supports an extension of the moratorium on Internet sales taxation at least through 2004

- Opposes taxes on access to the Internet

- Supports permanently banning Internet tariffs

- Supports meaningful, broad-based tort reform to protect our most innovative companies from frivolous and junk lawsuits

- Supports lifting the current limit on H-1B visas; believes long term solution to the shortage of high tech workers is education

- Called for reforming the high tech export control system by allowing

American companies to sell products in the international marketplace when these products are readily available in foreign or mass markets

Farm Policy:

- Would work aggressively to open markets for U.S. products and producers

- From this point forward, would not use food as a unilateral sanction or diplomatic weapon

- Called for emergency disaster relief, both through direct payments to farmers and through reforming crop insurance

- Supports tax incentives for use of ethanol

- Calls upon European Union to abide by the rules of the World Trade Organization and allow importation of genetically modified farm products

- Will ensure aggressive enforcement of antitrust laws and will move forcefully against any agribusiness entities that are conducting anti-competitive practices

- Supports reviewing and expanding the H-2A temporary agriculture workers program so that willing workers can provide much needed help to America's farmers

Trade:

- Supports restoration of "fast track" negotiating authority for the President

- Called for eliminating trade barriers and tariffs everywhere so "the whole world trades in freedom"

- Called for strict enforcement of anti-dumping and other unfair trade laws

- Supports expansion of NAFTA throughout the Americas

- Supports China's and Taiwan's admission into the WTO

- Supports revising export controls, to tighten control over military technology and ease restrictions on technology already available commercially

Social Issues:

- Pro life with exceptions for rape, incest and life of the mother
- Set the goal that all children should be welcomed in life and protected by law
- Supports parental notification, banning use of taxpayer funds for abortion, and banning partial birth abortion
- Supports efforts to increase adoptions
- Opposes doctor assisted suicide, believes the role of a doctor is to relieve pain and suffering, not to end life
- Opposes same sex marriage
- Make permanent the $5,000 adoption tax credit

Abstinence:

- Proposed spending at least as much on abstinence education as on teen contraception programs
- Proposed ensuring that faith-based organizations can compete for federal abstinence education grants
- Proposed studying the effectiveness of federally funded sex education programs

Affirmative Action:

- Opposes quotas and racial preferences
- Supports "affirmative access" to open the doors of opportunity through programs such as the Texas 10 percent plan, where those who graduate in the top 10 percent of their class are automatically admitted to any state college or university
- Advocates needs-based contracting and breaking down government contracts to smaller sizes to encourage entrepreneurship in all communities

Environment & Natural Resources:

- Believes environmental standards must be based on the best science, market-driven technologies can provide solutions, and government should encourage innovation and going beyond compliance

- Recognizes that global warming should be taken seriously but will require any decisions to be based on the best science; opposes Kyoto Protocol

- Supports moratorium against offshore drilling in California and Florida

- Opposes breaching dams in Pacific Northwest

- Supports conservation of land, wetlands and habitat, particularly by private landowners

- Supports protection of private property rights

- Reinvest in America's natural resources by fully funding the Land and Water Conservation Fund (LWCF) and guarantee a 50% share of the LWCF for state and local conservation

- Supports alleviating the substantial repair and improvement backlog facing our national parks, wildlife refuges and other public lands

Campaign Finance Reform:

- Supports banning "soft money" contributions from labor unions and corporations because members/shareholders have no say in how those contributions are given

- Supports enforcement of the Beck decision and enactment of effective "Paycheck Protection" legislation so union members have the right to decide whether to direct money to political activities

- Supports raising individual contribution limits

- Supports instant disclosure of contributions – was the first presidential candidate to voluntarily implement this reform with near-real-time disclosure on the Internet

Judges:

- Would appoint strict constructionists who would interpret the law, not legislate from the bench

Crime and Gun Laws:

- Supports stronger enforcement of existing gun laws, would provide more funding for aggressive gun law enforcement programs such as Project Exile in Richmond, Virginia

- Supports automatic detention for kids who commit crimes with guns and a ban for life on serious juvenile offenders from ever purchasing or carrying a gun

- Supports requiring instant background checks at gun shows by allowing gun show promoters to access the instant check system on behalf of vendors

- Supports law-abiding Americans' constitutional right to own guns to protect their families and homes

- Supports the current ban on automatic weapons

- Supports banning juveniles from possession of semi-automatic "assault" weapons

- Supports increasing the minimum age for possession of a handgun from 18 to 21

- Supports banning the importation of foreign made, "high-capacity" ammunition clips

- Supports voluntary safety locks

- Opposes government mandated registration of all guns owned by law abiding citizens

- Opposes legalizing "medical" marijuana

- Opposed granting clemency to 16 FALN terrorists. Believes that, as a nation, we must have zero tolerance for terrorism

Civil Justice:

- Supports meaningful, broad-based tort reform
- Called for Y2K tort reform

11

Biography

George W. Bush is the 46th Governor of the State of Texas. Now in his second term, Governor Bush has earned a reputation as a compassionate conservative who shapes policy based on the principles of limited government, personal responsibility, strong families, and local control.

During three Texas legislative sessions, Governor Bush has worked in a spirit of bipartisan cooperation with state leaders and members of the Texas Legislature to enact historic reforms to improve public schools, put welfare recipients to work, curb frivolous lawsuits and strengthen criminal justice laws. In his five years in office, Governor Bush has delivered the two largest tax cuts in state history – nearly $3 billion dollars – to Texas taxpayers.

Governor Bush's first priority is the education of children. He has worked with the Legislature to increase the State's share of funding for schools, restore local control, strengthen the State's accountability system, give parents and students greater choice of schools, end social promotion, and foster competition and creativity through charter schools and an expanded menu of educational opportunity. His most profound goal for Texas is that every child will learn to read by third grade and will continue to read at grade level or better throughout public school.

George W. Bush was born July 6, 1946, and grew up in Midland and Houston, Texas. He received a bachelor's degree from Yale University and an MBA from Harvard Business School. He served as an F-102 pilot for the Texas Air National Guard. He began his career in the oil and gas business in Midland in 1975 and worked in the energy industry until 1986. After working on his father's 1988, presidential campaign, he assembled the group of partners that purchased the Texas Rangers baseball franchise in 1989 and later built the Ranger's new home, the Ballpark at Arlington.

He served as managing general partner of the Texas Rangers until he was elected Governor on November 8, 1994, with 53.5 percent of the vote. In a historic re-election victory, he became the first Texas Governor to be elected to consecutive four-year terms on November 3, 1998 winning 68.6 percent of the vote.

Governor Bush won 49 percent of the Hispanic vote, 27 percent of the African-American vote, 27 percent of Democrats and 65 percent of women. He won more Texas counties – 240 out of 254 – than any Republican other than Richard Nixon in 1972 and is the first Republican gubernatorial candidate to win the heavily Hispanic and Democratic border counties of El Paso, Cameron and Hidalgo.

Republicans won all 17 statewide races on the ballot in 1998 because of Governor Bush's coattails. Republicans, including eight women, two Hispanics, and an African American, now hold all 27 statewide constitutional and judicial offices.

Governor Bush and his wife, Laura, a former teacher and librarian who grew up in Midland, reside in the historic Governor's mansion in Austin with their 18-year-old twin daughters, Barbara and Jenna, their dog, Spot, and their three cats, India, Cowboy and Ernie.

Governor Bush is a Methodist and has served on the boards of various charitable, business, and civic organizations.